My Dogs

And How They Shaped My Life

Best wishes –
Jude Heumel

WD

WELLDONE
PUBLISHING

Saint Paul, Minnesota

My Dogs

And How They Shaped My Life

Jude Heimel

WellDone
PUBLISHING

Saint Paul, Minnesota

Published by WellDone Publishing

Saint Paul, Minnesota

ISBN: 978-1-7322527-0-7

Library of Congress Control Number: 2018905853

Book Shepherd, Design and Editing: Joanne Sprott
Dog Illustrations: Bernie Heimel
Cover Design and Logo: Marilyn Solo
Author Photograph: Christopher David McLaughlin

Printed and bound in the United States of America

Dedication

In memory of Sister Benignus, my fifth grade teacher, who led me to believe I wrote good stories and...

In appreciation for all teachers who help children to read and write.

Contents

Introduction

Dear Reader,

   There are eight dog stories here. These are stories about wonderful dogs, sometimes heroic, sometimes hilarious, always loyal and affectionate companions. My dogs. Two dogs were my childhood companions and six dogs are from my adult years. My experiences with these dogs shaped my life. I learned lessons about values, relationships and myself.

My dogs have helped me through some tough times. If there is just one thing they taught me, it is to take difficulties one step at a time and trust the process of life. By taking just one step at a time while going through divorce, doing physical therapy or coming to peace with a new disability, I have made progress. I've come to think of this as "dogged resilience."

These are also stories about me and my feelings. My feelings have been sometimes joyful, sometimes sad. I have been worried, scared, happy and thoughtful. I shared my feelings with my dogs and now I share them with you through my dogs' stories.

Perhaps you've said, or you have heard someone say, "I'm never going to have another dog. Sadie (or Gus, or Sugar) just died. I'm not going through that again. It felt horrible." The sadness of losing one's friend and loyal companion can hurt so much that you deny yourself months and years of enjoyment. That's what I did.

After I lost my loyal childhood friends, Paddy and Turk, I shut down my feelings and denied myself thirty years of the pleasure of being with a dog. That's why you will find such a large gap between my last childhood dog and my first dog as an adult. Yes, during that time I was productive, I enjoyed myself, and I even had times of great happiness as well as times of sorrow and disappointment. I had friends and lovers. I did interesting and useful work. I cared about people; people cared about me. At some level though, I was closed off and I didn't even realize it. By closing off my feelings in one area of life, I dampened my capacity to feel the highs and lows in other areas of my life, too.

I invite you to walk into these pages with all of your senses and with your heart wide open. Perhaps, you, too, have been damaged in some way by disappointment, lost dreams, and the incredible hurts possible in life. I hope you will enjoy these stories, taking whatever life lessons they afford you. And I wish you a deep connection with a companion dog that encourages you forward one step at a time.

Jude Heimel

June 2018

Saint Paul, Minnesota

Paddy, My Wonder Dog

September 5, 1958 – December 10, 1961

Do you remember your childhood well? I have the usual snatches of memories; some are of the good times, some are of the bad. In all of them, though, one childhood friend and companion stood out in a shimmering light, just like the red-gold of his Cocker Spaniel coat. Paddy, my Wonder Dog, braver and more courageous than the dogs of any of the animal stories I read as I grew up in suburban and then rural Minnesota. Let me tell you his story. It starts in

June of 1958.

The summer of the year I turned ten was one of reading, reading, reading. I lived to be inside of my books. My head was filled with the heroic stories of the dogs I was reading about. Lassie, White Fang, Balto. The original Rin Tin Tin. Max, Chips and other war hero dogs—World War II was still a recent memory for many authors describing the exploits of soldier dogs. There were also family dogs, pet dogs that saved their people, maybe from fire, maybe by pushing a child out of the way of a careening vehicle. Sometimes they were hurt themselves in the process. Oh! How I loved those stories of courage and loyalty!

Every Saturday morning, I rode my bike to the library three miles away. I loaded up the basket attached to the handle bars with eight, ten, even twelve books at a time and pedaled home with my treasures.

I read lying in the grass in the front yard. The perfect spot was in the shade of an evergreen tree where I could lie on my back. One time I found a nest of tiny, baby rabbits hidden in a small indentation in the grass. I covered them back up and tiptoed away. I remember the grass being about three inches high and luxurious. My father was always late to mow it according to my mother's preferred schedule; when he did he also wore short shorts, and she was aghast at his "indecency." Eventually, she stopped asking him to cut the grass.

I yearned for a dog who would be my closest friend. Every night when I readied for bed, I prayed to God to bring me a dog. I wanted the type of bond between human and dog that I had read about. I wanted a pal to tell my innermost thoughts to, to confide my feelings and worries to, and to be someone whose love and affection were steady and sure.

I don't mean to convey that I was a lonely child, though. I actively played with the neighborhood kids. I remember I insisted on being "Belle Starr, Queen of the Outlaws," in the games we played while crisscrossing the neighborhood. I did have two siblings: my older sister, Deanie, and my younger brother by two years, Ed. Still, I yearned for a dog, my dog.

My family always had dogs when I was growing up, but the dog was the family dog, or my father's dog, not mine. There is a difference.

Foremost among the dogs that passed through my family's life, I remember Bingo, a black and white Springer Spaniel that clearly was my dad's dog and trained for hunting. Nevertheless, Bingo took his family responsibilities seriously and served as guardian for us kids. As shown in our old home movies, Bingo watched my every move as a toddler, and when I went too close to the street, he would stand between me and danger. With the dog in front of me, I was distracted from whatever ideas of roaming I had, and in one scene, I joyfully clasped my arms around his neck and hugged him, sitting down sharply from the exertion. After Bingo bit the mailman that had tormented him for years, though, he had to leave.

I watched a series of dogs come and go after that, never staying for long. I don't know why that was. I don't know where those dogs came from. People were casual about their dogs in those days.

My dad was the one who always brought the dogs home. They were full-grown dogs, no puppies. I remember a German Shepherd, and a black Lab. I think sometimes it was a country dog that its owner thought would do better in the city. No chickens in the city, perhaps. Maybe we were just taking care of someone's dog for a week or two while they were on vacation. Maybe my dad was trying to replace Bingo and never found the right dog. He certainly didn't have time to hunt anymore, much less train a hunting dog. He was occupied providing for his five-person, later seven-person, family.

Although I remember walking several of the dogs on leashes occasionally, it was clear to me that these were not my dogs. I had no say in their training, or lack thereof. I did not feed them. I did not know when or why they came or why they went. I don't remember them ever being in the house.

That changed just before Christmas when, with no forewarning, my father brought home a golden-red Cocker Spaniel puppy. I was in the kitchen when he came home and put the puppy in my arms with the admonition, "Take good care of this little guy."

"For me? For me, Daddy? Is this my dog?"

"What are you going to name him?" my dad asked.

Oh, wow. My dog. I had just been reading a story about Irish immigrants. A young man was called a "Paddy." I pictured the puppy as a young man with red hair and a rakish air, a cap on his head, his hands in his pockets, whistling a tune. "Paddy. His name is Paddy."

With the puppy declared to be mine, I took over every aspect of his care. I was unable to convince my mother to allow him to sleep in my bedroom, so I made his bed in a cardboard box and layered it with old towels. The box stayed in the kitchen. I found water and food dishes. I pestered my parents to buy the best dog food they could find.

With the few dollars I had earned from doing my chores, I rode my bike to the drugstore and bought a red cloth collar for Paddy. I already had a leash used with the previous dogs, and I walked with the puppy, following him around the back yard. In the house, Paddy could only be in the kitchen so we were outside a lot. There were a few months of school left. The puppy grew. I doted on him.

When summer started, Paddy was nine months old and ready for serious training. I spent hours every day with him. Sometimes he sat in the grass with me as I continued my reading habit, this time, "How to Train Your Puppy." I combed and brushed him until his coppery coat gleamed.

Every day I snapped the leash on him and we walked around the yard. "Sit." "Stay." "Heel." We were together every day. I was with my best friend. That was a golden and green summer. It was glorious.

At the end of the summer, my parents told me, "We're moving." When I learned we were moving to the country I was delighted and oh-so excited! We kids loved the idea. Mother hated it.

Our new place in Lake Elmo was a "gentleman's farm." I understood that to mean no hard work of tilling the soil and harvesting crops. It was all pasture land, divided into two large pastures with a third, smaller one, too swampy to use. All in all, it was about twenty acres.

The house was big, huge actually. It had been on the market for some time. The dilapidated buildings included the three-story house, a three-car garage, an old ice house, a large, falling-down chicken coop, an open-to-the-elements hay barn, a two-story cattle and horse barn and a large workshop and tool shed. The furnace room and cellar were under the house but had an outside entrance. It was lakefront property with a long sweeping lawn down to the lake.

The house had formerly been an institution, a country hospital. My father probably got a good deal on it, and it served his desire to better himself. He had worked in the restaurant business for years, working his way up from butcher to bartender, manager and finally owner. To him, the house represented success for a child of immigrant parents.

We didn't see much of him except some on Saturday and then on Sunday for church and family day. His work had him coming home in the early hours of the morning while we were asleep and waking long after we went to school. Mother was our parental interface ninety percent of the time—at least until we were old enough to join Dad at work.

Mother hated the new house and was deeply resentful of our move. She missed her suburban lifestyle near her lady friends and their lunches out. She had loved dressing up to "go somewhere fancy."

It's only now when I recollect her comment on our first trip down the long driveway of the new house, "Oh, John! There are so many windows!" said with surprise and displeasure, that I realize that that was the first time she had seen the house. My father had sold the old house and bought the new one without consulting her.

Paddy's and my life changed when we moved to the country. Before, it had been hours of playing together outside. Now Mother demanded more of my time. She had her hands full with the new addition to the family—Bernadette, now a one-and-a-half-year-old toddler. So it was chores for me inside the house and out. Paddy accompanied me on any outside chores, like weeding in summer or snow shoveling in winter. Since Mother only allowed Paddy as far as the kitchen and then only on the most brutal of Minnesota winter nights, we had less time together.

The new locale and my busier life also gave Paddy an opportunity to get into trouble. As my brother, Ed, and I walked home from school one day, we heard a shotgun blast. "What was that?" We ran the remaining way to the house and saw the neighbor farmer, a middle-aged Norwegian bachelor, chasing a running-full-out Paddy. Ed and I made it to the house at the same time as Mr. Anderson. Paddy was already on the porch, cowering under the yard furniture.

"That damn dog killed my best laying hen! I'm going to kill him!" Fortunately Mr. Anderson hesitated to shoot onto the porch. Dad had not yet gone to work, and he came outside to find out what the commotion was. I ran to Paddy and sheltered him with my body. That man was not going to shoot my friend! I don't know how he did it, but Dad talked the farmer into giving Paddy another chance. "We'll keep him tied up," I heard.

And so every morning before school, I tied Paddy up with a rope around a tree. Nevertheless, one day he chewed through the rope and got free. He must have immediately headed back up to the farmer's hen house, because this time he came home with the chicken, quite dead, in his mouth. I had read about what was normally done with a chicken killing dog. The prognosis was not good, but one technique was to tie the dead chicken around the dog's neck until the chicken rotted and the dog hated the smell of it. With some fumbling, I tied a rope around the chicken and managed to attach it to Paddy's neck. "Paddy, I hate to do this, but you can't kill Mr. Anderson's chickens. He will kill you!"

Paddy shook his body fiercely, trying to get the chicken off. With another shake the chicken and rope flew off and Paddy ran onto the porch and hid under a low chair. Now I was panic-stricken. If I didn't teach Paddy to refrain from killing chickens, he would be shot! There's no room in the country for a chicken-killing dog.

I ran after him onto the porch, and in a frenzy, I reached under the chair to yank him out. I had to punish him! Frightened, he growled and snapped at me. That brought me to my senses. I rocked back on my heels and tears flowed down my cheeks. "Paddy, please. You cannot do this. I don't want to lose you."

Paddy crept forward and into my lap. This time I clasped him tightly and cried with my arms around him. We sat that way for a long time. When I released him, we walked back to the chicken still lying on the ground. I picked it up, shook it at Paddy and said a firm "No!" Together we walked to the outside trash bin and I threw the chicken in. Paddy never chased chickens again.

After we moved to the country, my younger brother, Ed, and I remained close, but we spent less time with our older sister, Deanie. She went off to high school early and spent most of her Saturdays working in Dad's restaurant. Mother seemed to be fine with this arrangement. "Take her with you," she had told Dad one Saturday morning shortly after we moved. "She's your daughter, after all." Deanie was Mom's stepdaughter and Mom seemed to prefer that she not be around.

Ed and I spent our after school time and Saturdays doing chores on the farm. We went back and forth by bus to the Catholic school in the next town. Paddy accompanied us on our trek to the bus stop. He waited with us and later found his own way home. When the bus returned us to that spot on the highway, Paddy would be there and walk Ed and me home.

To keep the grasses and weeds in the front pasture down, my father bought a flock of sheep soon after we moved in. The man he bought the sheep from, Mr. Hanson, also bought and sold horses. Hanson's property had little acreage and ours had unused pastures, so my father and Mr. Hanson worked out an arrangement whereby the Hansons would keep horses on our property and his sons would take us kids riding. It worked out well.

We did have a lot to learn about sheep raising, though. Our "citified" approach of coddling the ewes by keeping them in the barn during that first Minnesota winter and feeding them plenty of oats killed off a number of them. Turns out they needed exercise and fresh air.

By early spring, we ended up with several orphaned lambs. During their early days, we kept them in the kitchen near a heated radiator and fed them by bottle. Paddy, when Mother allowed him in the house, kept a friendly but inquisitive eye on them.

Later in the spring, I got permission from my parents and the school authorities to bring a lamb to school. I corralled Wooly, one of the orphaned lambs, put a collar on him and squeezed him into a dog crate. Dad drove me in the station wagon to school that day. Instead of "Mary had a little lamb, little lamb…," that day it was, "Jude has a little lamb, little lamb, little lamb, and she brought it to school today." During recess and lunch, I walked Wooly on a leash on the front grounds of the school. Drivers of passing cars registered their surprise with a smile and a wave.

Occasionally, the sheep found their way out of the pasture. Once they got as far as the railroad tracks, and several of them were killed. After that, Paddy and I kept a special eye out, checking to make sure they were all in the pasture. Despite our best efforts at refencing, the sheep continued to get out periodically. When that happened, Paddy and I went looking for them and often found them in the nearby fields of Mr. Anderson. Not good.

With broad arm waving, whistles and encouragement, Paddy and I communicated sufficiently to herd the sheep. I gestured with my arm far to the left and cried, "Paddy! Move 'em!" as I, too, moved to the left. Although he was a block away from me, Paddy dutifully trotted to the left. The sheep were in front of him, and startled by his movement, ambled in that direction as well. In this way, calling Paddy toward me and waving him away, we lurched with the sheep back toward home. Ed held the gate open and the wayward sheep scampered into the pasture.

Since I was frequently occupied with school and housework, Paddy became a more independent dog. When we did have time to just be together outside, he was as likely as I to decide what we would do: go in the barn and look for mice or check on the baby lambs. Mr. Hanson also sometimes had us go out to hunt for a particular horse to bring in and saddle up. That was great fun.

By fall, the spring lambs were strong and husky. They played together for hours, especially the young rams. They would face each other, butting heads with a bang. And then again: Bang! Bang! I shuddered at the sound. The young rams did not have horns, but the tops of their heads, starting almost immediately above their eyes and past their ears, was solid bone and hard as rock. This bone structure formed a nice flat "battering ram" to work with.

One day after school, Ed and I were doing chores. Ed was in a corner of the sheep pasture near the house, watering the sheep. We had lightly fenced off a small section of the pasture where one line of fencing met a second at a ninety-degree angle, forming a corner where we fed and watered the sheep separately from the horses.

I was in the garden weeding when I heard Ed scream. "What was that?!" I looked up and around for him. Ed was crying. "What's the matter?" I cried. Then I saw that Wooly, one of the young rams, had cornered Ed up against a large wooden fence post. I saw Wooly butt him just as he did his fellow young rams. Ed screamed again. Wooly's head was rock hard, and he was butting Ed in the groin again! To get to Ed, I had to run out of the fenced garden, through its far gate and around to the front pasture to crawl between the rails of the fence. Ed screamed again and continued his crying. I ran as fast as I could, but Paddy got there first.

As I ran up to the fence, I saw Paddy lunge at the young ram's shoulder, bumping him hard. But the ram was almost three times his size, and Paddy's effort was not enough to stop him from his fun. Paddy lunged again, jumped high and grabbed Wooly's ear, biting down hard. That finally stopped him and he turned on Paddy who had tumbled to the ground after his high jump. While Paddy dodged the charging ram, which was not operating in fun anymore, I was able to help Ed gingerly climb between the fence railings.

Mom appeared and escorted Ed, crying and sniffling, up to the house. When next I saw him, he had one of Mother's Kotex pads protecting his bruised groin. He took it easy for several days.

Meanwhile, Paddy had had no problem keeping away from the ram. Once Ed and I were out of the pasture, he trotted over to me and lay down at my feet, panting. I was so proud of him. He had figured out the situation and had courageously rushed in to save Ed. "Good dog, Paddy! Well done!"

No one else seemed to think too much of Paddy's heriocs. Nevertheless, I did, and I told him so that night as we sat side by side on the dock down by the lakefront. I put my arm around his shoulder as we gazed out at the lake.

"Paddy, you are wonderful! You are just as good as Lassie!" That incident was when I first knew I had a very special dog.

Not long after that, my father brought home a second dog, a two-month-old black Labrador puppy. We named him Mike. Paddy took Mike in hand and began to teach him some of the basics: sit for your meal, walk with Ed and Jude to the bus stop and return home without too much loitering.

The puppy seemed to enjoy country life. One day he was out in the front pasture, lost in its sights and smells. That day, Mr. Hanson brought over a truckload of new horses. The current group of horses jockeyed around the gate to see who was coming in. As the new horses were unloaded, a lot of shuffling around occurred, and a run began, with the horses neighing and snorting, bucking and rearing as they raced after each other. The pasture formed a large oval with an old apple orchard at the far end. The apple orchard was separately fenced, but open at both ends. The horses began galloping the outer loop of the pasture oval. They swooped up into the orchard and raced toward the far side. It was a sight to behold.

I think I noticed it first. "Look! Mike is out there!" The puppy had wandered onto the sandy track that the horses used when they galloped out of the orchard, down the hill, and out to the flat land below.

"He is going to get killed! The horses will kill him!" None of us could get to the puppy in time. "Mike! Mike! Get out of there!" Our calls were in vain.

At my side, Paddy stood up, saw Mike and scooted under the fence. He sprinted toward the puppy. Could he make it in time? I swear he ran so fast that day that his ears streamed out behind him. But the horses were already in the orchard and coming out fast. Mike was exactly in their path.

Paddy rushed straight through the tall grasses, unerring in his mission to rescue Mike. He reached the puppy, picked him up by the scruff of the neck and half carried, half dragged him to the side of the sandy track, just far enough to be out of the horses' way. The horses swept by, some bucking, all running flat out. Paddy and Mike were safe. We were jumping and screaming, clapping and laughing.

That was when I named him Paddy, the Wonder Dog.

By December of 1960, life had settled into a nice country rhythm. I had just had a good time at Maggie and Darlene's. I didn't often get included in that group of local girls, but during this evening out, Maggie had confided to us about boys and her dates. Meanwhile, Darlene, a tomboy like me, sliced potatoes with a pocket knife, and we fried them on the wood stove. I never imagined you could do such a thing!

As I left their home and headed for the shortcut home across the frozen lake, I slid just a bit down the snowy embankment. The frozen, rippled ice of the lake was oddly less treacherous than walking downhill on snow. A full moon shone on the lake and its orderly cluster of ice fishing houses. The square shanties were set up in rows as a village, with three streets running parallel to each other. The "main street" provided a nice path directly to the lakefront of my family's property. It was a nice walk in the moonlight across the lake, up the long hill to my house and then in for the night.

As I walked along, I smiled remembering Maggie's stories. Would I ever have boys seeking me out as they did her?

The ice fishing houses were dark that night; the bitter Minnesota cold that froze the never-fathomed, deep lake with ice two to three feet thick had sent home even the hardiest of fishermen. The snow cover on the lake crunched under my feet, and at times I could hear the ice crack. It didn't mean the ice would open up under my feet, but the sounds were as if the lake, even frozen, were alive.

As I walked past one ice house toward the next, I noticed a dark shadow flit between the same ice houses but one street over. Had I seen something? What could it have been?

I passed the next ice house and once again, in the space between the two buildings, I saw a dark, low shape matching my pace. At an ice house or two before the end of the village, I saw the shape more clearly. A large dog was padding along, pacing itself to me. It's stalking me! I realized, and in the same instant I knew that one of the Johnsons' wolf hybrids had escaped its enclosure and had come to the ice house village to prowl. Now, I was its prey.

I recognized the situation I was in, but I didn't know what to do. I was almost at the edge of the ice house village. Whatever protection those one-room cabins had provided me was almost gone. I had about 100 feet of frozen lake yet to cross with no cover, and then when I reached our property there would still be no cover and no weapon until I reached the house, which was up a steady incline, perhaps a block long.

What to do? Go forward? Run for it? As much as I wanted to run, I knew that was the wrong thing to do when being stalked by a hunter with such an ingrained prey drive.

Go back through the village and go to Maggie and Darlene's house? If the wolf dog followed me, as he surely would, I would face the same situation on the other side of the lake. I was as frozen as the lake with my indecision. The wolf hybrid was slowly approaching me between the remaining ice houses.

Then an orange blur of fur flew out of the darkness and in a fury hurled itself onto the wolf dog. "Paddy! No! Come back! You'll be killed!" My first reaction was terror for Paddy. My 30-pound spaniel against a 120-pound wolf dog!

Then I heard him clear as day—"Quick! Run for it! I'll follow!"

I understood. I was to go and to go fast. I ran faster than I ever had, my legs pumping up that hill. I reached the doors closest to my path, swung them open and ran into the living room. I held the door wide open. I had to make a safe entry for Paddy, even if the wolf dog tried to get in, too. Not a moment later, Paddy raced in, sliding to a stop a few feet beyond me. I slammed the door, my heart pounding. "My God. What just happened?"

I sank to my knees, crying and calling him. Paddy climbed into my lap and I sat back. I felt him all over. Blood on one ear but he appeared to be all right, only panting heavily, excited.

My dog partner had just taken on a wolf to protect me. How had he even known I needed help? I knew he waited for my return when I was at school. He had been on lookout for me.

Paddy, Paddy. What an extraordinary dog! Paddy, my Wonder Dog.

In December of the next year (1961), I had come home by bus one Saturday morning after a school event. Deanie and Ed and Mike (now a full grown Lab) were there to meet me. "This is odd," I thought. "Where's Paddy?" I asked cheerily, still flush with the pleasure of being with friends.

As we walked home, and with some hemming and hawing, Deanie and Ed told me that Paddy had been killed by the wolf dogs. My heart dropped. I couldn't believe it. Paddy, gone?

Ed explained that he had been in the barnyard when Mike ran up to him and started biting his sleeve. At first Ed had thought he wanted to play, but biting was not allowed. Mike ran toward the pasture, back to Ed, back toward the pasture. Ed had followed, still puzzled.

He'd found Paddy lying in the snow with his head gashed open. Paddy was already dead. From the tracks, Ed had pieced together what happened. The three wolf dogs had come into the pasture and chased the horses. One horse was cut from running into the barbed wire fence. Paddy had tried to stop them and they'd turned on him. Mike had run for help.

They explained that Mom had told them to tell me that Paddy had run away and that that was why he wasn't around. It was for my own good she had said.

That evening Deanie, Ed and I huddled together with the television on in front of us. "Shh! I hear Mother coming." We stopped talking about Paddy and his horrible death. We focused on the television set. I continued hugging Mike.

Mother entered the room behind us. She stopped just inside the doorway and took in the scene of her children banded together and showing no interest in her presence.

I turned my head and looked at her. She glared at me. "I'm glad he's dead," she snapped. "You loved him more than me." With that she wheeled and stalked out.

I was stunned. We remained quiet as we heard her go down the stairs. She was soon out of hearing. "'I'm glad he's dead!' Did you hear that? How could she say that to me?"

At that moment I hated her. The grief I felt at the loss of my beloved friend and companion was like nothing I had ever experienced before. I was thirteen years old. I had no tools to handle this. I had no help either.

Ed and Deanie tried to be supportive, but they had never had strong feelings about a dog or any other animal. They couldn't comprehend what I was feeling. When I did show a glimmer of the hurt and loss I felt, it was frightening to them. Children themselves, they didn't know what to do.

Mother allowed no talk about it. We were to act as if Paddy had never lived. The other prevalent attitude, exhibited by my father, was, "He was just a dog. Get over it." That was how we lived the post-Paddy days and months in the house.

I continued to hold Paddy in my heart, but alongside the love I felt for him, a deep resentment was growing against my parents. I did not understand the silence enforced by them. Paddy had died heroically, and no one cared. He had proved himself time and again in his efforts to protect me and my family. Why couldn't we talk about him?

I believe this misguided act on the part of my parents was supposed to protect me from my grief. As I've learned since about the fear of death, acting as if it isn't happening is more useful in protecting others from my grief. Strong emotions were not allowed in our household.

As for myself, I felt that I'd let him down. I hadn't stood up for him. I'd let my mother bully me into not being an embarrassment by showing deep feelings. I let her jealousy rule my behavior. I kept quiet, I did not speak up. And I felt shame for my silence. I loved Paddy with all my heart, yet I couldn't stand up to my mother and say so.

As spring came and the ground started to thaw, I began to dig Paddy's grave. I could only clear a few inches of frozen ground at a time, but I persisted. Paddy was still frozen, still lying in the cardboard box he had been thrown into in the corner of the barn. I had been afraid to move him. I was afraid Mother would learn that I had.

I asked no one to help me bury him. This was my final act for Paddy.

On Easter Monday, I finally had a sufficiently deep hole. I brought a soft, woolen winter scarf, a favorite of mine. I went to the barn and picked Paddy up in his box. He was still frozen, so there had been no deterioration, but he was matted and dirty with dried blood.

We got to the grave site, and I wrapped him gently in the scarf. I was crying and my nose was running. I laid him in the grave I had made for him. I placed shovelful after shovelful of dirt on top of him until I could no longer see him. I continued until there was a slight mound over his burial spot.

Good-bye, Paddy. I continued to cry as I marked the spot in my mind. Finally it was time, and I walked away.

December 1974, thirteen years after Paddy's death; from my journal:

Inexplicably, I have awakened in tears several mornings in a row. I don't remember my dreams. I don't know what is going on with me.

I have puzzled on it for several days. Nevertheless the morning tears do

not cease. I seem to have no control over these feelings of great loss and sorrow.
What is the matter with me?

After several more days, it occurred to me that this was exactly the time of year that Paddy had died. I looked it up in my journals. Yes. It was exactly that. December 10, 1961. I noted that it had been thirteen years since his death and that I had been thirteen at the time. This was some kind of special anniversary, I realized. My body knew it even if I had not sensed it consciously.

I hadn't grieved well for him when he died. That time of grief had been taken away from me. I had been forced to hide it. Then at twenty-six, it was able to come out. Finally, I honored Paddy by honoring my grief.

Now, 55 years since Paddy's death, I mourn yet again. I grieve for my faithful companion, my loyal and courageous friend. My first dog. Paddy, my Wonder Dog.

The life lessons I learned about grief from Paddy's death were not healthy ones. I learned about how difficult it is for the people around the grief-stricken one to be supportive. Even with the best of intentions, what is one to do? How is one supposed to act?

I learned that one must not show their feelings, not strong love, not strong sorrow. I kept my grief inside of me and hardened my heart. I soon knew well the feeling of resentment, which stayed with me for years and became part of an easily triggered, insidious pattern. I thought, "I'll show you. You'll never see my loss and hurt. You'll never know how I feel. You'll never know how much you have hurt me." That was my coping mechanism. Not a good one in the long run.

I never forgot my mother's comment that she was glad Paddy was dead. She was unable to reach out to her daughter who was so hurt and dealing with death for the first time in her life. Instead my mother could only think of herself. She went inside herself and served up something black and mean. I learned then that my mother was not my friend. Her feelings and wants and needs always came first. My grief could not trump her jealousy; she wanted the love and attention I had showered on Paddy.

I realize now that my mother was a woman consumed with anger and resentment. She was forty-two years old at the time of Paddy's death. She had ended up with a total of five children to care for. She had thought she was done with her child bearing years, yet she had just had another child, a boy, nine months before. Bernadette was almost four, still too young for school. Mother lived in the country away from family and longtime friends. She had a huge house to manage. She believed her husband was fooling around with other women. She wanted someone on her side, to see her life the way she saw it. She wanted that from me, her thirteen-year-old daughter. She did not have the wherewithal to step out of herself and help me deal with my grief. I forgave her much later, but I never forgot.

From Paddy's life and companionship, I learned just the opposite of the emotional lessons my mother had taught me. "You stand by your friend. You have their back. You are loyal and true." Paddy taught me what it was like to have a friend, to be a friend.

I can't help but cry as I write this. What a magnificent animal Paddy was! All heart and smarts. He was brave to take on that ram. He was smart to figure out what was going to happen to Mike, the puppy, at a future point if something was not done immediately. He was heroic to take on the wolf dog to protect me. He was courageous to take on the whole wolf pack to protect the horses. He never hesitated. I remember him and his bravery when I am procrastinating over a loathsome or frightening task that needs to be done. I feel his encouragement to act.

Paddy taught me about courage and loyalty. From my love for him and then my grief over his death, I have learned lessons about feelings that have lighted and shadowed my life since. I have learned to recognize my mood of resentment and in some instances, even to shift out of it. I have had dogs since Paddy, although never one so heroic. My dogs, good dogs all, have led my way out of the insidious pattern of resentment. That didn't happen easily, or soon, though. First, there is the story of Turk, my beautiful Golden Retriever.

Turk, My Golden Boy

Late Winter 1963 – unknown

Turk and Taffy arrived about a year after I buried Paddy. By that time, Mike, the black Labrador that had tried to bring help to Paddy when the wolf dogs attacked him, had disappeared. I thought someone had picked Mike up because they had heard the university was paying $35 for any dog sold for use in research experiments. Dad said some hunters must have taken him because he would be such a good dog for hunting. All we knew was that one day Mike wasn't home for dinner and we never saw him again.

April 1963 journal entry: *I played with the pups today.*

Early the next spring after Paddy's death, Dad brought home two Golden Retriever puppies. They were litter mates, one male and one female. I got to name them. I named them Turk and Taffy. At three months, Turk was already handsome and the deep golden color commonly thought of as a "Golden." Taffy was thin and long legged, scrawny actually, and more of a red gold color. These were dogs to stay; they were the family's dogs, but I was the one who took care of their feeding and grooming.

June 1963 journal entry: *We don't see too much of Mom and Dad. They are working every night now.*

There had been other significant happenings in our household during the ensuing year; matter of fact, most everything seemed changed. We did still live at the big house in Lake Elmo that Dad had bought in 1959, with its several pastures for horses and sheep. Dad was still working long hours at Northwood, the supper club he had bought. Now, however, Mom was working full time, too at the small corner bar in South Saint Paul that Dad had originally sold on a contract for deed, but which had come back to him. So now both Mom and Dad were working, and we kids were at home by ourselves.

We "kids" were also reduced in number. Deanie, my older sister, never had been on good terms with Mom, and she left home during that summer. I was now fourteen, to be fifteen at the end of the summer, when I would start tenth grade. That would be my first year at Stillwater Senior High.

Ed turned thirteen during that summer and would start eighth grade at St. Michael's Elementary School. "The babies" were now ages five—that was Bernie aka Bernadette, and two—that was Mike, the human (in my mind named Michael Patrick after the dogs, Paddy and Mike).

With Mom and Dad working, doing the chores and taking care of the little kids was up to Ed and me. That summer we got Bernie and Mike up, fed them three meals a day, did the laundry, cleaned the house, kept the yard in shape with mowing, trimming and weeding, took care of the animals (sheep, horses and dogs), and put the little kids to bed.

I don't remember really minding all the work. It just seemed like what had to be done, so I—we—did it. Mom didn't like working in the neighborhood bar. Ed and I had other things we wished we were doing but the little kids didn't know any better; it was just the way things were.

I didn't mind Mom not being around since I still resented her for her cold attitude about Paddy's death. I also took some satisfaction in running the household and, in my opinion, doing a better job than she did.

Being fourteen, I'd discovered that boys were really important, and there were plenty of them around. We had a paper boy who walked to the house and delivered the paper, Ron Svenson that was. After one year on the school district bus going to junior high for ninth grade, I was now better known to the kids in town. A certain small set of boys my age and a bit older would, one or another, accompany Ron on his rounds and end up hanging out at our house, sometimes through dinner. Plus the Hansons had two boys my age. They would pop in frequently to take care of their horses. Since I was a bit "boy crazy" at this time, having this company made home and the work there more fun.

A couple of things happened that summer that taught me lessons about life.

Mom was home for the first one: One morning in early July, I came upon Turk and Taffy. They were stuck together, back end to back end. I tried pulling at them by pushing their heads, then rumps, in different directions. I couldn't get them to budge, so I started yelling for help. Mom stuck her head out the window to say "what is going on?" When she did figure it out, she yelled angrily at me to get in the house "right now!" (Taffy had puppies nine weeks later.) When I figured out what was going on, I was embarrassed, curious and more knowledgeable.

The second story was a bit different: One afternoon that summer, Ed, the boys visiting that day and I were outside with Taffy and Turk, fooling around. Near the driveway, next to a small hummock where the horses were unloaded from the pickup truck, was the well. It was a deep shaft covered by a well cover (much like a manhole cover).

A couple of the boys took to showing how strong they were, lifted the cover off the well housing and set it aside. They were as surprised as the rest of us to see at the bottom of the shaft a large number of snakes all tangled together.

The boys started hollering. Everyone gathered around. A few of the boys got some sticks and threw them at the balls of snakes. Turk and Taffy started barking like crazy. I felt snake fear rise in me, and I wanted to hurt those hateful snakes. They were on my property, after all! I could do what I wanted to them! We gathered rocks, then small boulders, crashing them down onto the snakes.

By the time we were done, every snake was dead. A quiet settled over us. I asked, "What kind of snakes were they, anyway?"

Someone said quietly, "Garter snakes."

"Garden snakes? Are they good for the garden?"

Soon after that the fun was over. The boys dispersed, and I took Taffy and Turk down to the dock. I sat with an arm around each of them, dangling my legs over the dock and did some thinking.

"Those snakes weren't harmful." I said to them. "I didn't stop to think about what type of snakes they were. I just saw 'snake!' and I was scared. There were so many of them!"

I explained further, "I felt scared and then I felt hatred. I was angry and I hated those snakes because I was scared of them." This was quite a realization for me. I felt like I had stumbled onto an important life lesson: Fear can lead to hatred and then to anger and violence. When it is all over, there may not have been anything to fear in the first place.

Turk nuzzled me; he and Taffy seemed to agree.

Turk and Taffy regularly helped us manage the animals in the pasture, in this case for a horse culling.

"Go get Diamond—and her colt. Bring 'em in. I got someone coming to look at 'em," Mr. Hanson told us when he came over one day. Diamond was purported to be an Arabian, and her colt looked like it, too. Diamond was a dark gray with black markings. The colt looked just like her, only a little lighter. I whistled for Turk and Taffy; they would accompany me. Darrell and Howie Hanson gathered up halters and along with Ed, we headed out.

The big pasture contained by far the majority of the twenty acres of our farm. There was no spot in the pasture from which you could see every section. The best place for organizing ourselves for a search was the old oak tree, so that's where we gathered. It was centrally located along the spine of a ridge that ran down the center of the pasture, basically dividing the pasture into two long sections, each with several different types of terrain. To further the difficulty in finding a particular horse, the herd didn't all stay together. There were small groupings of them—two or three, maybe as many as five. Where they rested depended on the weather, where other horses in the pecking order were located and what time of the day it was.

"Let's check everything behind us and in the roadside pasture first," I instructed. "Ed, you go to the back near the chicken coop and just make sure none of the horses are there. I'll take Turk and Taffy to check out the rest of the roadside. That leaves the difficult terrain pasture for you, Darrell and Howie. Let's get back here as fast as we can to decide what to do next. If someone has found Diamond, say so and we'll all go there with the halters. If not, we'll go to the far end of the pasture. Sometimes they go all the way to the other side of the green shed."

With Turk and Taffy, who were seven to eight months old at the time, I walked through the meadow and bog area. They didn't roam on their own as much as Paddy and Mike had, but they loved to hike the horse pasture with me. They didn't chase the horses, but they enjoyed the sights and smells of squirrels and rabbits.

We were all back in a few minutes. "Nope."

"No sign of them."

"Not at my end."

At that point, we left the oak tree and headed out along the ridge to the farthest end of the pasture. Turk raced ahead. I glimpsed him rounding the far side of the shed. He was out of sight for a moment and then he came galloping back, straight to me as if he had a message to share. Sure enough, on the opposite side of the shed were Diamond and her colt. No other horses were around, which made it easier to walk up to Diamond and slip a halter onto her head. Then Darrell walked Diamond to the corral with us and her colt following.

By working together we were able to do the job in less than fifteen minutes. If it had just been one or two people searching while sticking together, they could never be sure the sought-for horse hadn't slipped behind them along one of the trails they couldn't see. And it was fun to work together. Even Turk added his part. That was a lesson about teamwork that I have always remembered.

In the fall of 1963, I entered tenth grade, Ed started eighth grade, and Taffy had her puppies. Taffy had always been sickly, though, and having the puppies seemed to take the last spark out of her. She was also less than one year old, too young to give birth and be a mother. The puppies were sickly, too.

There were four. One was born dead and not fully formed; another one although fully formed was also born dead. Two were alive, a beautiful white-cream colored puppy and a golden brown one. Unfortunately, the cream colored male developed fits and died. Only the brown female lived. We named her Penney, but she didn't stay with us long.

October 1963 journal entry: *I had a fight with Mom about the dogs. Dad took Taffy and Penney to the Humane Society.*

Later that fall Dad brought home another black Lab. I named him "Stat" after hearing the word used in a hospital program popular at the time. It means "fast!" Now the family dogs were Turk and Stat. I didn't have the type of time with them that I had had with Paddy that glorious summer before we moved to the country, so I never trained them to the extent I had Paddy. Turk and Stat came when called, knew to sit before they ate and didn't jump on people. They didn't learn to herd sheep as Paddy had, for example, but they were good dogs and well behaved for what was asked of them.

Meanwhile, I had started high school in Stillwater. I threw myself into school my sophomore and junior years and got good grades. I kept my Catholic elementary school friends, and I made new friends. When I could, I participated in extracurricular activities like drama and debate that didn't require requesting a ride home from parents.

The corner bar in Saint Paul was sold during that time, and Mom went back to being a stay-at-home mom. Ed finished eighth grade and then began going to Saint Paul, "the city," to Hill High School. He got a ride there from a neighbor man and then found his own way home, seven to eight miles, by a combination of hitchhiking and walking. Bernie went to the local elementary school, but Michael was still too young for elementary school. He may have had some pre-school classes but I don't remember.

At home I had chores and the dogs, Turk and Stat. Turk, with his upbeat, happy-go-lucky golden personality, had wriggled his way into my heart; he was definitely my dog by that time. Stat was of uncertain ownership; just the family dog, perhaps. For some reason, I believed that both dogs couldn't be mine. I don't know if Mom said that Stat was Ed's, for example. I don't know if I just thought I couldn't have it all.

Stat spent most of his time with Turk and me, though. When we had free time, the three of us would be down at the dock, watching the water, hanging out far enough away from the house that I could convincingly say, "But I didn't hear you."

In this way, we passed the summer of 1964 and then another year arrived and a sudden shift in our lives.

August 1965 journal entry: *We're moving.*

When I was told the news two weeks before I was to start my senior year at the high school, I wailed, I cried, I begged.

"Please. *Please!* Can't I stay with the Wendt's (neighbors) with my dogs? They said it would be all right. I will babysit for them all the time—for free!... It's just for one year....It's just for nine *months!*...Please! This is going to be my best school year *ever.*"

And indeed, it was going to be a great school year, and one for which I had worked hard. I was to be editor of the school paper, a position I was thrilled to have, and I had already begun planning how to improve the paper's coverage. I was a contributor to the school's literary magazine, and I had written two stories during the summer. A contract for the honors program was sitting on Dad's desk. It would include advanced history and English, with Fridays off for special research projects! I had been looking forward to the new school year. We would be *seniors!*

But my parents would not budge. With the short time frame before moving and starting a new school, I didn't have time to say goodbye to my friends. It was like I just disappeared and magically appeared in a new high school where I knew no one. Lunch was the hardest at the new school. I had no one to sit with. When I sat near some girls, I would get a hello and a smile and then they went back to talking amongst themselves about things I wasn't familiar with. It was agony, and all the while I was thinking, "If I were at my old school, I would have lots of friends!"

I was devastated to lose the senior year I had so looked forward to, but at least when I came home from the new school Turk and Stat were there. There was a lake less than a block from our new house. I walked Turk and Stat along the lakefront grassy park every night after dinner. The dogs gave me solace, especially after a difficult day at school. I told them about my day. They always agreed with my side of the story.

They also served as an entree to meeting people. Sometimes, I saw school mates at the lake and we began saying tentative hellos. As I got to know people, occasionally a new friend would walk around the lake with me, Turk and Stat.

As I settled in to the new school, I began to focus on my academic activities. In a few classes, I made a name for myself as "the new girl, the smart one."

Two months into the school year, I came home from school, grabbed the two leashes and looked for the dogs. "Mom! Where's Turk and Stat?"

"Your father took them to a nice farm. They are country dogs, Jude. They'll be better off there. Don't be selfish."

I couldn't believe it. I don't remember wailing or begging at this news. This was more horrible than changing schools my senior year. It was like it was after Paddy died. I felt completely betrayed. I felt alone. Again, I had lost my best friend, two of them this time. Again, I had no chance to say good-bye. No warning. It was just…done. I went upstairs to my room and stared at the ceiling. I cried myself to sleep. I didn't go downstairs until it was time to go to school the next morning.

I was outraged at the unfairness of my situation. For the next few days, I operated on automatic pilot. I did my chores at home by rote and then went to my room without speaking to anyone. At school, I just went from classroom to classroom, following the schedule. My head hurt. My legs were heavy. I was depressed. I felt helpless, hopeless. I knew there was no changing my parents' minds. I hated them.

I resolved to not give them the satisfaction of knowing how much I was hurt. They took me away from my last year of high school where I would have excelled academically and been on the path for college. They took away my dogs and all of my friends from the old school. My resentment burned. I resolved to not be concerned with academics that year. I would hang out with the fast crowd. I resolved not to love another dog just to have it taken away from me. I hurt more than was bearable. I wouldn't let it happen again.

A week later, on a Friday after dinner, I completed the after meal clean up and swept the kitchen floor. I emptied the dust pan into the waste basket in the kitchen closet at the back door. I saw that the basket was full. I gathered the bag inside the basket and tied it tight. I turned to the door behind me to put the trash bag into the larger barrel in the garage. As I took the top off of the barrel and placed the trash inside, Turk and Stat rounded the garage corner at a full gallop. They raced across the floor and into my arms.

"Oh my God! You found your way home! Oh! My darling, darling, darlings!" I sat on the floor sobbing. Turk and Stat jumped all over me trying to get into my lap, under my arm, trying to get as close to me as possible. They were excited, too, and very, very pleased with themselves.

How had they found their way back to me? And to the house we had been at for such a short time!? When I thought about it later, I realized that no matter from what direction they had come, they had had to cross four-lane highways, many residential streets and presumably had started at a farmer's fields some distance away. They had found their way home traveling a path I had never taken them on.

I cried from happiness now. I was so proud of them. I had never loved them more. Surely this proved that our home was where they wanted to be. This was where they *should* be.

◇◇◇◇◇◇◇◇◇◇◇◇◇◇◇◇◇◇◇◇◇

November 6, 1965 journal entry: *Mom has called the dogcatcher. He's coming at 2 pm to pick up Turk and Stat.*

I wasn't even home when the dogcatcher came. By that time, I had taken Deanie's place working Saturdays at Dad's restaurant. From my work station in the kitchen, I watched the clock above the door. I imagined my two well behaved dogs doing as they were told, waiting for the strange man to lead them away. Or perhaps they were scared as they were loaded into an unfamiliar truck. Perhaps they even remembered what happened the last time they were driven away from our home. The clock struck two. I said goodbye in my heart to my two dear friends.

In the days and months that followed, I shut down my feelings. I never saw Turk and Stat again. I don't know what happened to them.

Turk had become my best friend, and to prove his loyalty to me, he had led a heroic journey home for him and Stat. I had loved him. I had loved Stat. Losing Turk and Stat—twice—was like the experience of losing Paddy. I believed that my mother had intentionally hurt me. I believed that she had intentionally taken away what I loved most. This revived my childhood resolve to not show my feelings, yet I was consumed with grief and anger. I was afraid to show those feelings, though. I feared being punished. We were not to show strong feelings in our household. My feelings of grief and anger eventually became resentment, and finally, resignation.

◇◇◇◇◇◇◇◇◇◇◇◇◇◇◇◇◇◇◇◇◇

My parents were reasonable people. They did not, however, in any way, shape or form see a dog as a best friend. They were practical. Two large dogs, both of them breeds requiring a lot of exercise that was easily accomplished when we were on a farm, did not have their needs met by a daily stroll around a lake.

Perhaps to them I exhibited the histrionics of an over-indulged 1960s teenage girl. A dog was just a dog for criminy sake. My mother had finally gotten out of the country and out of the huge house that required so much upkeep. My father now lived a few miles from where he worked until the early hours of the morning. No longer was there the very real possibility that he would fall asleep at the wheel while making the long drive home. My brother no longer had to hitchhike home from his high school; the city bus route went right past his school. The younger kids changed elementary schools and had no problem making new friends.

These are things I can imagine now as being part of their thinking. Nothing like this was explained to me at the time. In my family you didn't explain adult decisions even to almost grown daughters. And, in truth, it probably wouldn't have helped me. I was immersed in my feelings. Feelings of hurt and loss, grief and betrayal. My lesson was to not feel, to shut down. I came to understand that life can be hard, hurtful.

After a few years, that childhood resolve of, "I'll show you. I'll withhold my feelings. I'll hide my true self," became my adult pattern in times of difficulty. I got to the point that I couldn't identify to myself my shadow-side feelings. Numbness took over. I received regular messages from my body— vomiting, diarrhea, muscle spasms in my back—that the feelings had not "disappeared," but had just gone underground.

Still, in the midst of all that loss, I learned that the only thing to do is to pick yourself back up and continue forward. That, I think, was part of the work ethic my family uncomplainingly exhibited. I continued to hide my feelings, but I was able to act and contribute. I learned that regardless of the hurts, attacks, snubs that might occur, there is a core inside of "me" that cannot be touched unless I allow it to be.

During the Turk and Stat time, I had several experiences that led to the formation of other patterns and values. I remember the snakes where my fear of the unfamiliar and strange led to hatred. And then chagrin as I realized how fear had led to violence. I remember the old oak tree where I learned that working as a team is more effective than as an individual.

I recognize now that in my childhood I chose to hide my feelings and that this decision eventually led to being unable to identify and acknowledge my feelings and to think that they had disappeared, or so I thought.

I had an active, rewarding work life for the next thirty years. But I never opened my heart to a dog partner during that time. It took me a long time to acknowledge that the way a dog touched me and was willing to be my best friend was a beautiful thing. And that it is worth the pain that is part of the relationship. But that is Lil Bear's story and that didn't take place until my fiftieth birthday.

So for now:

Goodbye, Turk.

Goodbye, Stat.

Thank you for the experiences we lived through and the dog values you helped teach me about loyalty and unconditional love. I hold you in my heart forever.

Lil Bear, My Black Collie

September 19, 1998 – August 3, 2006

My love for dogs was reawakened by Lil Bear, a black collie puppy put into my arms when I was fifty years old. That started a time of great joy for me.

I had just met Phil, a charming, handsome man who was the sole proprietor of an auto restoration business. His home, complete with dogs and cats, was in a sleepy little Hispanic town southwest of Albuquerque and just 250 miles north of the Mexico border. The house was large and sprawling, cozy and comfortable, with shade from lofty cottonwood trees.

The year before, I had left corporate life as a road warrior in a Fortune 50 company and had begun my own business providing consulting and team facilitation in strategic planning and process management for research organizations. Phil was spontaneous, fun, high energy. He sparked up my rather dour, overly work oriented life.

Phil had three dogs. Arrow, a Malamute, was the alpha dog of the pack. Sheltie appeared to be a purebred Shetland Sheepdog and was a bit of a ditz. His third dog, Snoopy, the Beagle, was his own man, and other than Arrow, no one had much influence over him.

Phil had just divorced, and he had a two-year-old son, Tim. Although Tim spent most of his time with his mom, he was a regular visitor to the house. Phil was determined to be an attentive father even though living separately. I came to consider myself Tim's friend and an adult role model, but not a parental figure. He and I got along famously.

That first summer Phil and I were together, I watched Sheltie be gallantly courted by a shaggy black dog of mixed breeding. On my fiftieth birthday Sheltie gave birth to four puppies. I didn't know that the little black male puppy was going to be my dog until three months later when, instead of selling him as he had planned to do, Phil put him in my arms as a Christmas present. "Here. He's yours." It was like a switch turned on. "You are giving him to me? He's *my* dog?"

It felt wonderfully right to have "my dog" again, and I stepped into the relationship wholeheartedly.

Phil was astounded by my careful and caring attitude toward Bear. "Wow. Why didn't you say you wanted one of the puppies? I would have given you one right away."

"I didn't know," I said, a bit amazed myself.

For years I had not had a lifestyle that would accommodate a dog. Because of my work, I had been a frequent traveler with no one at home to care for a dog while I was gone. At several points in my career, I had been away from home far more than I'd been present. And when I was home, I had worked long hours, much longer than a dog should be left on its own. It didn't make sense to me to have a dog only to kennel it for more time than not. I did not mention and I wasn't really aware that I had also cut that interest out of my life based on my childhood losses. I didn't want to feel that grief I had experienced before of losing my dog.

Now I had a new lifestyle with support from others. I was so excited about my relationship with Phil that I told my sister, Deanie, "Even going to the WalMart is fun with this guy!" Within a year Phil and I were engaged. The engagement provided formality to what had quickly become a closely entwined relationship, and it was time to announce that closeness to the people around us.

Bear grew up to become a handsome fellow. Lean in his younger years, his black, collie-like coat fell beautifully in waves on him, with extensive feathering on the back of his legs and on his plumed tail.

Arrow helped introduce Bear to riding in a car, and he was soon calm and unafraid. I took him everywhere with me. In the back seat of the car, he found his own system for buckling up. He slid between the back of the driver's seat and the front of the back seat and tucked himself in the space on the floor with his head on the rear seat. He was so quiet in the back that sometimes I had to check to see if he was still there. I would reach my hand between the driver's seat and shift mechanism to touch him, and he would respond by licking my hand. "Yup, we're together," he seemed to say.

I took Bear to puppy obedience classes that a friend of mine had recommended. We went all the way through puppy, novice, and advanced novice. He even received snake training since our walks over northern New Mexico brought us into rattlesnake territory. The training definitely took.

A year after the class, Bear and I were walking down a main street in Santa Fe in front of the famous La Fonda Hotel with its gorgeous and expensive shops lining the interior first floor. My normally very obedient black collie stopped abruptly on the sidewalk. I could not get him to go forward. He would go sideways; he would return the way we had come, but he wouldn't go forward. I didn't know what to make of it. I knew there was something bothering him, but I couldn't for the life of me figure it out and I wasn't going to bully him through it. So, we crossed the street. I thought that might break whatever spell he was under. Nope. We got to an equal position on the sidewalk, and he locked his forelegs into a frozen position; he was not going forward. What the heck?! "Bear, come on!" I said in exasperation. Then I finally noticed what was troubling him, and I was astounded and very proud of him. A large truck was parked in the middle of the street with its Tommy Gate open, and several workers were unloading crates to carry into the La Fonda. The crates contained *snake*skin boots and belts. Bear knew he was not to go forward. "Good dog, Bear. We don't have to go this way at all." I petted him and rubbed him all over. What a good dog! Well done.

Bear was a happy dog. He loved everybody—cats, dogs, the neighbors, people he met on the street, even the little calf in the field across the street. But most of all, he loved me, and I loved him. It was so wonderful to have a dog again after thirty years! It was like all this pent up dog-love came flowing out of me, and he was the recipient. Of course he returned the love in kind. It made me happy just to be with him. Bear added an element of fun and joyfulness; he seemed to be saying, "Life is so exciting!"

Besides me, Bear's favorite friends were Arrow, Phil's Malamute, whom he followed around adoringly, and an orange kitten, Pumpkin, whom we brought into our entourage at only four weeks of age, after Phil and Tim found her abandoned at a local feed store and rescued her.

I think it was clear to Bear that his job was to be with me. He certainly followed me closely everywhere I went. If I changed rooms, he padded right behind me. If I got up in the middle of the night for a bathroom stop, he came along and flopped next to the wall until it was time to follow me back to bed. I've heard lots of people say their dog follows them like a shadow. I guess that's what Bear was, my shadow, my buddy, a constant presence when circumstances allowed us to be together. He had a very expressive tail, and he used it to indicate his readiness for whatever the next activity with me was. If he was lying on the floor across the room and I looked to him, he beat his tail on the ground. "I'm here. What's next?" he seemed to say.

Sometimes, though, my work did not allow me to take him with me. Perhaps I could not manage the round trip to work and back in one day, or perhaps I was working offsite for the client for a few days. I think at those times Bear felt he was off duty, and he would take the opportunity to wander off to "schmooze" as Phil called it.

One favorite activity of his was to visit Tippy, the neighbor dog. Bear would leave our yard to appear on the neighbor's doorstep. He barked. They opened the door to see what was going on. Bear walked in, crossed the house and stood in front of the far door that entered the back yard where Tippy was fenced. Lou opened the door and Bear went out to play, Tippy delighted to see him. This happened many times, although I did not know about it until long after.

When Bear was about a year old, Phil and I went away for a holiday. We didn't kennel the four dogs. Instead, Phil arranged for a friend to come by and feed them once a day. Other than that, the dogs were on their own. His three dogs were used to that.

When we came home from that trip, I saw Bear sitting under the cotton-wood tree. He didn't come to greet us as the truck pulled into the driveway. "Something is wrong with Bear." Even before the truck was fully stopped, I slid out of the cab and ran to him. Bear hadn't moved. When I got close to him, he tried to stand up but his hind legs crumpled.

"I'm taking him to the vet," I said. "I'm leaving immediately."

I took him to a vet in the next town that I had begun to use, Dr. Van Otten. Dr. Van Otten gave Bear a careful examination, but he didn't do any X-rays or other tests. He noted where Bear winced when touched and where he seemed to be OK. He thought that Bear had possibly been hit by a car. "He has a cracked pelvis. He needs about six weeks of rest. You must keep him confined and take only the most minimal, leashed walks for him to eliminate. He'll be alright." He carried Bear carefully to the car and we started for home.

I was uneasy. Somehow the effort that Dr. Van Otten had put into making his diagnosis and the bill for not quite $50 didn't seem to match the seriousness of Bear's injury. I turned the car and headed away from home toward another veterinarian clinic I had heard neighbors speak highly of. With the help of a vet tech, we got Bear into the second clinic. Several hundred dollars later and after X-rays and a blood test, the highly recommended vet said, "He has a cracked pelvis. He needs six weeks of rest. You must keep him confined and take only the most minimal, leashed walks for him to eliminate. Bring him back after the confinement period and I'll do another set of X-rays to make sure he has healed properly."

I learned a lesson from that experience and brought my animals to Dr. Van Otten thereafter.

When Bear was about two, Arrow disappeared. She was very old, and during the past year or so had faltered and rallied many times. During one of my work projects when I was away from home, Phil notified me that Arrow was missing. She never returned. I think she left the yard on one of her normal excursions in the neighborhood, but became disoriented and never found her way home.

Sheltie died soon thereafter. Because Bear was always with me, Phil and Tim acquired a puppy from a neighbor's litter. Muggles joined the family and became Phil's dog. He grew into a large, sable colored dog, always very serious and well behaved. A year later, Phil and Tim introduced a Rottweiler-Labrador bitch whom we named Paddy, after my childhood pet. I was able to introduce some of the same type of care for Muggles and Paddy as I had for Bear. I arranged to take Muggles and Paddy to the same dog obedience training program I had taken Bear to. All three dogs became snake-smart after the training there.

Bear, Muggles and Paddy grew very close. Snoopy ended up the odd dog out, a grumpy old man. Phil used to laugh and say that we had two packs.

One was the "Three Musketeers": Bear, Muggles and Paddy, and the other pack was Snoopy.

Evenings at our house were family times. Phil converted the old two-car garage that was his former workplace into a comfortable lounging area. The room now had huge overhead vigas, thick carpeting and mahogany wood paneled walls. A fifty-two-inch TV was set up across from two soft, white leather couches, matching hassocks and a large wood coffee table. A pool table was set up on one side and a quarter of the room was devoted to Phil's office. The dogs, all 240 pounds of them, lounged on the carpet.

I enjoyed those evenings in front of the big TV. Spread out around me was my family—Phil and Tim, Bear, Muggles, Paddy, Pumpkin. I had longed for a life partner, someone to plan my day-to-day life and my future with. Now I had one. I hadn't focused on a family as part of that desire but now I had that, too. I was happy.

One long weekend we took Tim and the Three Musketeers to Sedona, a beautiful spot in Arizona that Phil and I enjoyed visiting. While there we stayed in a lovely cabin on Oak Creek. On one of our hikes along the creek, we came to a deep pool and Bear, the water lover, jumped in. Paddy, still a puppy, but large, grabbed his tail with her teeth. Either she thought she was saving him or she just didn't want him to be ahead of her. Regardless, as she pulled on his tail, lifting his rear higher, his muzzle and face went under the water. When we stopped laughing, we were able to rescue Bear, who showed no animosity toward Paddy. Later, while playing in the red sand of a dry creek bed, six-year-old Tim said, "This is the best day of my whole life!"

Phil and I felt the continued glow of that sun kissed day in Sedona. A few months later, on a cross-country car parts buying trip, we enlisted a long-time friend of mine, also a minister, to marry us in Nashville, Tennessee. Bear was our witness.

After we returned and while I was on a business trip, Bear, as usual, went schmoozing. This time he was gone for five days, and I almost gave up hope of finding him. I was intensely involved in a multi-day workshop, so Phil didn't tell me Bear was gone until the workshop was over. I came right home. I drove for hours around the area, calling his name. Sometimes I stopped the car and got out to yell loudly across the fields or into the alleys of the strip malls. No Bear came in response. That night I went to bed without Bear sleeping on the floor next to me, thumping his tail whenever I awoke. I felt a hole in my stomach to think of no Bear in my life. During the next few days, I traveled miles, searching and calling his name.

Finally, Phil got a phone call. After a minute or two, he hung up. "That was Tim's mom. Tim thinks Bear just walked up their driveway to their house. She says it's a very bedraggled black long haired dog. She's not sure if it is Bear. The dog is very tired and limping." We hurried out and went over together.

Yes! It was Bear, although I have to admit he looked so much the worse for wear that I wasn't sure at first. He managed a thump of his tail when I reached him, and I knew that indeed this was my missing pooch.

As we drove away with Bear ensconced in the back cargo area, our route home took us over the railroad tracks several blocks from where Tim lived. "What's that?" said Phil. "There. See the metal clasp?" Puzzled, I dutifully got out of the car and went to the spot he indicated. My God! It was Bear's rolled leather collar with the tags still on it. The collar had been unclasped. It had not slid off Bear's head. We could only imagine that someone saw Bear, captured him and threw away his identifying information. I came to believe that Bear had successfully escaped from where he was being held and had headed for the closest familiar spot, Tim's house.

As Bear grew older, he curtailed his wandering ways. I had successfully lobbied for fencing in the yard, and we had become better at corralling the escape artist Tim called "Houdini." The three younger dogs were a tight pack, which may also have kept Bear closer to home. Sometimes we separated the dogs because Phil and I were in separate locations. Muggles would stay home, and Bear, and maybe Paddy, would be at the Santa Fe house that Phil and I had established at that point as our future retirement home. Now, it served as my office and overnight housing to provide me a closer drive to northern New Mexico clients.

When the three dogs were united once again, they would inevitably do their pack howl, much like wolves do. "The pack is back!" Phil would say. Bear would give his yip-yip-yip. Muggles, always so well behaved, hesitated to make much noise, but with encouragement, he barked joyfully. Paddy, with her deep bay, blended the noises into a harmonious howl.

It was at this time that Phil decided to get some chickens. I like fresh eggs, I like green chile chicken enchiladas, but to tell the truth, I am a bit afraid of chickens, especially the roosters. The chickens ran loose in the yard, and several times a day I had to mentally and physically prepare myself to run the chicken gauntlet to get from the front door, across the yard, out the gate and to the car. I hated it.

I don't know if Bear picked up on that or if on his own he would have decided that chickens were good eating. One time as Bear and I came back from Santa Fe, Phil ran out of the house, flung open the cargo door of the Subaru and reached for Bear. "You goddamn dog! You got another one!!"

I scrambled out of the driver's seat and ran around to the back of the car. "Don't you touch him! Get your hands off Bear!" In his fury, I didn't know what Phil would do to Bear, and I knew Bear would make no connection between killing a chicken yesterday and being beaten today.

Bear cowered as far away from the cargo door as possible. I pushed myself in front of Phil. He pushed me back. I stood my ground and with my eyes dared him to go through me to get to Bear. He backed down.

"Tie that dog up. I don't want him in the house. And he can't be loose in the yard." He turned and stalked away. I sagged and sat down on the floor of the cargo area. Bear crept into my lap. I was shaking. Bear was shaking. What had just happened? What would happen next?

Later that night, Tim whispered to me, "He beat Muggles, too." My heart sank. Muggles, so sensitive to being a good dog, always wanted to do the right thing. He would have been heartsick at having angered his master.

"He wouldn't have done it if he hadn't seen Bear do it!" Phil yelled from the kitchen, defending his actions. "It was just a rolled up newspaper, anyway." Tim looked at his Dad with surprise, and I knew it had not been a rolled up newspaper.

Again I took Bear with me whenever I could. At home, he was tied in the yard. He did come in the house when I was there and stayed by my side. Finally for some reason unconnected to me or Bear, Phil decided to sell the chickens and the chicken hostilities eased.

That incident, though, marked for me that things had gone downhill with Phil. I came to realize that the more my business succeeded, the more Phil seemed to resent me. I thought I had found a life partner; however, the partner side of things had become pretty unbalanced. I had become totally responsible for the finances of running the house—and there were now two houses including the Santa Fe retirement home that was also my office. Our arrangement was that I would pay the operating expenses since my income was relatively steady. Phil was to work on auto restoration and acquire the big chunks of money that would pay off the houses. I said to him, "My work funds you achieving your dream of having your own auto restoration business! That's what you said you most wanted. If you would just put more time into it, I know you would be successful."

Unfortunately, Phil wasn't making any progress on restoring any of the three cars that were in his workshop bays. When I pressed him, he said he needed helpers. We tried that for awhile with me paying for their labor. When one car was sold finally, the money I had put into the car was no way near recovered. Phil was able to sell parts from the cars and make small amounts of money, but he kept finding excuses to not do the restoration required to prepare a vehicle for sale.

Tim, too, was having his own problems with his father.

As Tim got older, he wanted to be with his friends more than he wanted to be with Phil and me. His friends lived in his mother's neighborhood. He didn't go to the same school as the few kids in our neighborhood. After awhile, I realized that Phil was promising Tim interesting activities if he came to our house, but he didn't fulfill those promises.

"Dad said we'd go to the new Harry Potter movie when I came this weekend. But we haven't. I'm going back to my mom's this afternoon. Now there's no time."

As this pattern evolved over time, Tim became more sullen and hostile. Stomping around the house, "accidentally" knocking knick knacks off the shelf, he would mutter loud enough for me but not his father to hear, "I *said* I don't want to be here. There's nothing to *do* here."

Tim's behavior around the house continued to get worse, and my relationship with him deteriorated as well. His father paid no attention to him. Eventually the routine was Tim watching TV in the family room and Phil watching TV in the bedroom. I was in between, satisfying no one.

One Fourth of July, my frustration with Tim peaked. Phil took us to see the local fireworks. Tim didn't want to see the fireworks with us. He wanted to be with his mom. She would have taken a carload of his friends to the fireworks. Phil and I were sitting in the front seats of the car with Tim behind me while we waited for the fireworks to start. We had left the dogs at home. The air was tense. I didn't know what had transpired between Tim and Phil during the day.

I heard a clicking sound behind me. Click…click…click. "Tim, what are you doing?"

"Nothing." Click…click…click. I turned around in my seat and saw with astonishment that Tim had a small switchblade knife. He was flicking it open and closed.

"Tim! Put that away!" Click…click…click . "Phil! What is Tim doing with a knife??" No response from Phil. A few minutes passed still with the continued click…click…click.

This time I turned completely around in my seat, fed up with both of them. "Tim. Give me the knife.!"

"No!"

"Tim. Give me the knife."

"No!!"

"Give her the goddamn knife. Quit it both of you!" And Tim reluctantly gave me the knife.

I was furious. Had Phil known about the knife? What was an elementary school boy doing with a switchblade knife? Was this something Phil was bribing Tim with?

Later I learned that Tim's mother had called her three children (two of them adults) together that afternoon to tell them she was getting married. The wedding was set for October. One of the older girls said she wouldn't come. She did not approve of her mother getting remarried. Tim was very close to his mother. I think her announcement upset him greatly, but he wouldn't talk about it.

Click…click…click.

At this point in my relationships with Phil and Tim, the best times were when I went up to Santa Fe to work for a few days, taking Bear and sometimes Paddy with me. Long hours working on difficult projects was less stressful than my home environment, especially when Tim was at home with us.

Whatever feelings Phil had about me being the breadwinner, gratitude did not seem to be one of them. He seemed to resent me being gone and leaving him without a wife figure at home. He became more controlling of my time, expressing jealousy if something good happened to me when I went out of town on business.

I worked long hours on my business trips, and yet I seemed to have to "pay" for being gone before I left and again when I returned. When I was home, Phil laid back, and I then became responsible for the family—Tim's visits, the dogs, two houses, maintenance of the several driver cars and encouraging Phil in his business. I kept thinking that if only I worked harder—at being a partner, wife, stepmother, business owner—I could make things better. Pretty soon I was in a constant state of exhaustion.

On one of my work trips to the Santa Fe house, I had Bear and Paddy with me for a few days. Paddy, now quite the big girl at 100 pounds and twice Bear's weight, had inveigled her way into our overnights away from home. At the close of the work day, we all piled into the car. Bear was in the cargo space, nestled with Paddy. Bear faced forward, his eyes on mine through the rear view mirror. Paddy faced backwards and kept an eye on the traffic behind us.

I had no inkling that anything was wrong with Bear, but that night he died. I was on the couch watching TV with Phil. Bear came over and lay on the floor at the side of the couch. After a few minutes, a TV commercial came on. I jumped up and said, "OK, poochies, let's go outside! Last call!" There was no movement from Bear. "Bear! What's the matter?! Bear-Bear, come!" I knelt beside him. As I put my hand on his side, he expelled his last breath.

What? What had happened?? Bear had just...died. There had been no warning. I couldn't believe it. I was hysterical, crying. Muggles came over and sniffed Bear, then turned and slowly walked away.

We wrapped Bear in a blanket. It was August, a hot New Mexico summer night. We agreed to lay Bear in the back of the Subaru until morning, when we would bury him in the yard, near Sheltie. Phil got up early and dug the grave. I had been up a goodly part of the night talking to and hugging Muggles and Paddy. Phil and I, Muggles and Paddy held a simple ceremony over the hole Phil had dug. With Phil's help, I laid Bear's body in the grave. Paddy came over and sniffed Bear. She watched intently as I shoveled dirt over Bear's body. I gathered and laid white stones in a pattern on the grave. It was done.

I tried to figure out what had happened to Bear to make him die so suddenly. He just lay down on the floor next to me and in a few minutes he was gone. I didn't know why it happened, but figured it was a brain aneurysm. I talked to Dr. Van Otten to confirm my suspicion, but he neither agreed nor disagreed. He did say, "What a blessing. I can't think of a better way to go then to lie down next to the person you love and go peacefully."

I told Phil, "I don't feel bad for Bear. He died a quick, simple death. I feel bad for me. I don't have my friend anymore."

I wrote in my journal that night,

He's gone! Just like that. I can't believe it. I am going to miss him so much. He was always by my side. He was always ready to do whatever I asked of him. Ready to go. Ready to stay. I'll never have another friend like him. Goodbye, my faithful friend. I will miss you so.

Later journal entries:

As I wake up, I hear in my mind, "I miss you. I miss you. I miss you." At first I am puzzled. It takes a moment to remember, to figure out who I am speaking to and why. It's Bear. He's gone.

I feel a different type of sadness today. More despair. His "goneness" is more final. I woke up with a feeling of hopelessness. The grief is monotonous, ongoing, constant. I miss you, Bear. I miss you so.

This has been a tough week. Feels tougher than before, but maybe that's just because it is now. Yet it feels like my despondence and grief has settled deep.

Bear's friends missed him, too.

Lou from next door came over to say how sorry he was to hear that Bear had died. He and his wife would miss "the little rascal." That's when he told me the story of Bear barking one sharp bark at his front door to be escorted through the house and out the back door to play with Tippy. "We loved Bear, too, Jude."

I know Muggles and Pumpkin missed Bear. He was best buddy to each of them. Their sadness was not as apparent as Paddy's, however. She was morose. She and I hung out together a lot after Bear's death. Now I brought Paddy to Santa Fe to work with me, where before it had been Bear and Paddy. Muggles wanted to come and be with me, too, but his job was to guard the house. When Paddy and I came back, I spent extra time with Muggles, combing and combing his double coat as everyone lounged in the family room. We both took some comfort in that ritual.

With Bear gone, my relationship with Phil really lost its luster. I hadn't realized that the joy I had felt being with Bear had spilled over to color my family life. Without him, the cracks began to show and grow wider. Deep resentment toward Phil began to creep in and fill those cracks. Funny to think that the little black collie with so much love was what had held the family together.

At age fifty, I had opened my heart to a man, and a dog. I felt the dog had done well by me. I was not so sure about the man. I felt a knowing that with Bear gone, our family was in danger of breaking apart.

Perfect Paddy

January 1, 2001 – February 12, 2010

Paddy, my beautiful Rottweiler. I dreamt about her last night. I was telling people how wonderful she had been. I was preparing to write Paddy's chapter. "Come, Paddy," I say to my dream dog, "Sit next to me. We have a story to tell."

There is a delicious freedom when, as a woman walking alone down a city street or a remote hiking trail, you are accompanied by a ninety-eight-pound Rottweiler. The protective fears I normally carry with me disperse as rapidly as a threesome of teens looking for trouble or a hungry coyote lurking in the underbrush. Paddy was perfect at assessing a situation and choosing which Rottweiler image to project. In the Subaru service department waiting room, she growl-purred her enjoyment to an older woman petting her belly who said, "I so miss my Rottie." With the two-year-old toddler at the football field grasping her front leg to pull himself upright, Paddy remained stoic, strong, unmoving until he got his balance and moved on. In the car when we were stranded on the interstate one dark night, her fierce and frenzied barking told the three drunken men approaching the car saying "we can help, lady" that their help was not required. She was the only dog I have ever had that would stop in her tracks and trot back if called off from chasing a rabbit.

I loved her. She was my Perfect Paddy.

When we first got Paddy, we gave her The Monks of New Skete puppy aptitude test. Paddy came out as a "1," best suited for guard work or as a police dog. Tim was six years old at the time. With Tim so young, I told Phil if we didn't gentle her by six months of age, she had to go. Phil worked with her every day, cradling her in his arms, crooning "sweet, sweet Paddy" and rubbing her belly. It worked.

Paddy became my dog for sure when Bear died in August 2006. Before that there had been some pretence that she was my stepson's dog. But Paddy was way too much dog for a young boy. Phil was the first to notice that Paddy had chosen to be my dog. "She follows you into every room you go into." With the spot at my feet already taken by Bear, Paddy chose to be guard dog and always positioned herself between me and the door.

Paddy and I became even closer in our common grieving over the loss of Bear. Bear had been her best friend. She missed him as much as I did.

My home life with humans was not going well. I was the breadwinner, yet Phil wanted me to be home more, not spending time in my office close to clients but eighty miles away from him. Also, it was a rough day's commute. I looked for a way to still make significant money but to be at home more. I decided the solution was to act on my longtime desire to formalize my executive coaching skills with certification training in order to augment my consulting and facilitation practice. As a certified coach, a fair amount of my work would be on the telephone. The perfect solution, I thought. I began the process of obtaining coach certification with a premier executive coach training school.

However, 2007 was an emotionally difficult year for me. Death and grief permeated my life. Bear was gone and both Paddy and I missed him. In January my first mentor and friend of thirty-five years died. In July my sister, Deanie, died, followed by my mother in November. So many deaths affected my mood, and I found it harder and harder to keep my efforts going on all fronts.

Phil was not supportive in my grief, nor was he supportive of me going to school. My argument that this was necessary as a way to still bring home high earnings without so much travel did not seem to satisfy him. He wanted me to be available to him "now." He wanted "his woman" at home, making his morning coffee, available to him during the day, and cozying up to him at night.

As the year-long coach training program went on, Phil's temper flared more and more. Often I found myself in my little home office with all the dogs huddled around me when I was on the phone with my study group or with practice clients. Tim frequently holed up there, as well. Phil would rattle down the hall loudly muttering, "You spend more time on the phone than with me!"

Phil still was not bringing in any money for our considerable expenses. A basic coping strategy of mine became "work harder and things will be made right." I worked harder and harder, not just at school, or with the consulting work but also in being wife, stepmother and homemaker. I was the last to bed and first to get up, and I was wearing myself out.

Of course I should have seen it coming. Phil found a girlfriend, and when I went on business trips, he sneaked her into the house to stay for the days I was gone. When I found this out and he proved unwilling to change, I threw a bunch of clothes into the back of the Subaru and along with Paddy drove up to Santa Fe to stay.

Paddy missed her pack when we moved to the Santa Fe house. Tigger, a beautiful, long-haired gray cat, already lived there, but Paddy wasn't used to being the only dog. I tried bringing her to the dog park, but she never "got" it. She saw no reason to run and play with strange dogs.

One day, as we ended our perimeter stroll at the large dog park and approached the gate to exit, I saw two dogs running, one after another. A small dog was in front and a white Standard Poodle a bit behind. "Just playing" was my thought until the small dog in a fear-inspired rush crashed into the fence and bounced back more than a foot. "Come on, Paddy!" I urged and I grabbed her collar to keep her close to my side and clear about my instructions. We ran to the small dog, a hairy Dachshund, and I positioned Paddy and me between the small dog and the poodle. I never would have done this on my own, but with Paddy at my side, I was brave. The poodle was viciously snapping and trying to get at the Dachshund. Paddy and I moved side to side, continuing to block the poodle. I saw two women almost a block away, one struggling to run toward us. "That must be the Dachshund's owner," I thought. The other woman lagged behind, in no major hurry.

The running woman grabbed her dog in her arms and hurried through the gate. She yelled at the poodle's owner but that woman was still too far away to hear. When the poodle's owner came up, I said, "Your dog needs some training. He was trying to kill that Dachshund."

"Oh no," she laughed. "He was just playing!"

I tried again. "Your dog wanted to kill that little dog and he would have if my dog and I had not intervened. Here's the name of a trainer that takes problem dogs. Go. Your dog is dangerous."

I don't know if the lady ever did seek training. I suspect not. I also suspect that the Dachshund owner now goes only to small dog parks.

It was about eight or nine months after Paddy and I left the marital homestead and established what had been my office as our new home that I first felt rested. The pace I had been keeping—managing two households along with Phil's auto restoration business and my consulting and coaching business, being a part-time stepmom, finishing school, grieving the deaths of my sister and mother—had worn me out. I felt settled enough then to think about bringing another dog into our household. Our search resulted in the arrival of Dancer, a year old, black and white English Pointer-Border Collie looking puppy. He doted on Paddy. She taught him the habits of the pack she had been a part of and still missed: Sit calmly for your dinner. Come when called. Don't bother the cat. Chase the desert lizards. Avoid cacti. Don't worry about fireworks or thunder. Ride quietly in the car.

The dogs were my greatest joy.

I was still under a lot of stress. The divorce from Phil was turning quite acrimonious. Nevertheless, I believed that we could and would decide our breakup in a logical, fair, relatively amiable manner. However, Phil was a "one for you, two—or three—for me" kind of guy. I kept hoping that some fairness would enter the agreements and decisions. Then the mediator said to me, "Just pay him and run."

When the time finally came to sign the divorce papers, I was ready to be separate from Phil. Nevertheless, I keenly felt the loss of my dream to have a lifelong partner. I had been almost fifty years old when Phil and I had met. I had put too much of my dream onto the relationship and never saw him clearly for who he was. Instead I looked through a veil of hopes and illusions, wishful thinking and plain old denial. The night I signed the divorce papers, I cried long and hard. It was more for the loss of my dream than for the loss of Phil, specifically. I sat on the floor, one arm around Paddy, one arm around Dancer, sobbing. Occasionally I reached for the toilet paper roll and blew my nose. Other times, I just wiped my face on my sleeve. Paddy turned to me, licked my face. Dancer whined, uncomfortable with the show of emotions he didn't understand.

When I woke up in the morning, the hearing in my right ear was gone. It never came back.

In addition to the divorce, the fall of 2009 was a difficult one for me financially. My two major organizational clients both experienced payroll snafus lasting several months. I did not receive the pay I was owed. There were many assurances—"next week, for sure"—but they were not fulfilled. I missed one mortgage payment, then two. Phil had promised me that as soon as his inheritance from his mother's estate came in, he would pick up payments on his house as ordered in the divorce decree, but until then, I had to take over the payments if I wanted the mortgage paid up to date. When I pushed him for just some contribution, he got fiercely angry with me, yelling, "Don't you understand the pressure I'm under! My mother just died!" I paid what bills I could. However, I couldn't keep up. Once again, I was frazzled and exhausted. Once again, Phil contributed nothing.

By winter, I knew I had to rest up. I wanted to spend a significant period of the Christmas–New Year holiday time with my siblings, their spouses and the many friends I still had in Minnesota where I had grown up. I couldn't take Dancer and Paddy with me, and there was no way I could pay for their kenneling.

I had been delighted to care for Phil's dogs, Muggles and Kuriboh, earlier in the fall while he and his girlfriend had gone on a trip, and now Phil offered to care for Paddy and Dancer for as long as I wanted. I could go for two-and-a-half weeks. I decided to take him up on the offer. I made plane reservations, left and I was having a wonderful time when my phone rang as I was grocery shopping with a Minnesota friend. I saw it was Phil. I said to my friend, "I think I better take this. I hope nothing's wrong," as I answered the phone.

Chat. Chat. Chat. Dancer cute stories. I didn't get the sense of anything important until just before the end of the five- to six-minute phone call. "But that Paddy," he said. "We had to barricade her in the family room. She peed at the front door."

"Peed? She never pees in the house. Maybe something's wrong with her. She peed at the front door?" I had a sudden realization. "She must have been standing there for hours! She was trying to signal that she had to go out!"

Irritated that his story had raised my ire and not sympathy for him caring for my difficult dog, he added, "Well, maybe something is the matter. Last night, she got all wobbly. You know like Arrow used to do. She couldn't walk. But then by this morning she was fine again."

I didn't know what to say to this. "Well, keep me posted. Let me know the littlest thing that happens to her." We hung up.

I returned to New Mexico soon after and immediately after the plane landed, I got my car from the airport parking lot and drove to Phil's house to pick up Paddy and Dancer.

I waited at the front yard gate for Phil to open the door of the house. Paddy and Dancer bounded to me and I too was oh-so-happy to see them. After a quick hello, Paddy went directly to the Subaru hatch back door. She was ready to go home.

Glancing over at Paddy, I thought, "Oh, that's interesting. Paddy is really ready to leave." I took a moment to say hello to Phil's dogs. I hugged Muggles, who pressed himself next to me and exuberantly petted Kuriboh, who was all "wiggle-butt." Forcing myself to turn my back, I left Muggles and Kuriboh in the yard and assisted Paddy and Dancer into the Subaru. "Thank you for taking care of my dogs, Phil. Goodbye." I called out as I headed to the driver's seat.

"Hey! Paddy didn't even say goodbye to me!" He complained. "Well, we're all loaded in the car." I said in her defense, "Thank you. Goodbye."

For the past eight months, Paddy had had to share me with Dancer, and now I had been gone for a considerable stretch of time. I decided to put Dancer in doggie day care for a day and have a "Paddy Day," just her and me.

All that day she had my full attention. Some of the time I lay on the couch reading, my arm dangling off the edge of the couch and easily reaching to scratch her belly. We strolled around the lot, with her sniffing at the rabbit trails. I drove us into town and we walked on a cleared pathway. Paddy did not want to go far and she lagged behind me. When we came to a bench, we sat, enjoying the sun.

One morning, less than a week later, much as usual, I let Paddy and Dancer out for their first outing of the day. I made coffee for myself as I waited for them to return to the front door. I heard Paddy's gentle, one scratch signal at the door and I let them in.

I went into the kitchen to prepare their kibble. I turned from the counter with the two bowls. Dancer was at my feet in the kitchen and I set his bowl down. Paddy was sitting in the dining room. "OK, Patty-cake. Here's your breakfast."

Instead of striding toward me as she normally did, she scooted. She used her front legs to pull herself forward, but she couldn't get her back legs up. "Paddy! What is the matter?!"

I encouraged her to walk. She couldn't. I examined her carefully. Her face had a goofy Paddy grin. She didn't seem to be in pain but she could not move her back legs.

A bit hysterical, I called the Santa Fe vet's office. I told them to be prepared to help me get a 100-pound, partially paralyzed Rottweiler onto an examining table.

I wasn't sure how I was going to get Paddy there, but first I had to put Dancer somewhere safe while we were gone. I filled a water bowl and hastily locked him in the outdoor ten-foot by ten-foot kennel I had already established. I came back around the corner and saw that Paddy had gotten herself out of the house and had scrabbled down the front steps. She was waiting for me in the yard.

We were halfway done! But how was I going to get her into the car? I opened the rear hatch door. "Paddy, we have to get in the car." By this point, I had started to cry. "We're going to get you some help." Paddy tried to jump in and bumped her chest on the ledge. But this was enough to get her front legs up. I don't know how we did it, but somehow, with her pulling with her front legs and me lifting her butt, we got her in the cargo area. I slammed the door, grabbed my car keys and we tore off.

A burly vet tech was waiting for us. He wrapped Paddy in a blanket, gently lifted her and swiftly carried her into the closest examining room. It was already set up for us.

Our Santa Fe vet, Dr. Pete, rushed in and began to examine her. "There's no blood, no obviously broken bones. I have to do some tests. I can sedate her and take some X-rays. I'll know more this afternoon."

I left for home to check on Dancer and to cancel my afternoon business appointments. I headed back as quickly as I could, which was still too early for the test results.

The vet tech took me in to sit with Paddy. The cage they had for her was very large, so I crawled in, too, and sat cross-legged next to her. Paddy put her head in my lap and I stroked it gently. "Paddy, please get well. I need you. Dancer needs you. We're not done yet. Paddy, please don't leave me. Paddy, please stay with me."

I tried to control my tears but nevertheless they kept falling, and soon a Kleenex box was handed to me by one of the kennel workers.

I stayed in the kennel with her for more than an hour while Paddy slept with her head in my lap.

Finally, the vet came out to us, "I have the test results. Would you like to hear them?"

We went back out front to a client room. One wall was lit up with two X-rays. Dr. Pete and I stood in front of them; I looked at them, but I didn't know how to read them. He said words. I didn't understand the technical terms. I asked questions. Finally I got it. He didn't know what the problem was.

"It could be cancer. It could be something pinching her spine. It may be a blood clot. We can't see anything from the X-rays that would cause her rear legs to be paralyzed. You could take her to Albuquerque and get an MRI. That would show more. Maybe enough. That would help the diagnosis, but we are still left with the question of treatment."

I felt faint, but there was nowhere to sit. "I have to sit down."

"Of course. Tony! Bring in a chair!" the doctor called before continuing, "Sometimes a dog does recover the use of their legs. If you don't do the MRI, I suggest keeping her here for a few days. We'll keep the IVs going, keep a close eye on her. This could get better."

Of all the options, a blood clot along her spine was the most favorable possibility. I understood that—and the treatment would be living on a blood thinner for the rest of her life. That would not be a problem. That would be good.

I told him that Paddy had had some sort of episode a month prior. She had been all wobbly. Hard to get her bearings and walk. Trying to think of every possibility, I asked, "Could my other dog have done this? He jumps and pulls on her."

"No. No, his play, or even fighting would not have done it. Has she had an acute trauma?" I looked at him in confusion, so he explained, "Has she been kicked? Hit?"

"No! Of course not!" I exclaimed.

The doctor said that this was *not* normal deterioration along her spine. We settled on the IV course of treatment, but even then, he kept asking whether she had had a trauma. He said maybe the trauma happened before and was only triggered recently.

I was overwhelmed. This had happened so quickly. That morning everything was fine. I had sung a good morning song to Paddy and Dancer. We were happy.

Oh, Paddy, my Paddy.

I was aghast at the costs. And I was ashamed that I couldn't pay them. $1500 for an MRI! $3,000 to $4,000 for further diagnostic testing. Then treatment. At what cost? Enormous.

My emotions and reason were at war with each other. "Whatever it costs!" I wanted to scream. "Make her better! Fix her. I need my girl!"

But my reason said, "Paddy is nine years old. That's old for a 100-pound dog. The costs just to diagnosis the problem are thousands of dollars. You *cannot* rack up big bills you can't pay. You're just coming out of a divorce and that lawyer is not paid yet. You are in a probate battle with Phil's mother's estate and there are enormous legal costs there. You need hearing aids. You don't know how you are going to pay next month's mortgage."

Blind with tears, I OK'ed the vet's recommendation to keep her for a day or two. They started her on blood thinners and steroids to see how she would respond.

I went home. I took Dancer out of the kennel and hugging him, I sobbed. "What am I going to do? What am I going to do??"

I visited Paddy two or three times the next day. I sat in her huge crate with her head in my lap. In the morning, she who was normally always hungry was not interested in the treats I brought. I could tell she was pleased to have me sit with her, however.

When I came home, Dancer went to the hatchback door of the Subaru and waited for me to open it and for Paddy to come out. Dancer was bewildered. "Where's Paddy?" he seemed to ask. I had never left him home alone before. I wondered if he could smell her on my clothes. I wondered if he could smell her sickness.

Phil called and I told him that Paddy had another episode and that she may be dying. "I want to see her. Don't let her go until I can get up there," he said.

"When do you want to come?" I asked numbly.

He dithered and I figured out it was because he was trying to determine when his girlfriend would not be home. He didn't want her to know. "This isn't about you and your convenience, Phil. This will be about whatever is best for Paddy." I hung up, making no promises.

That night I woke up suddenly. I had been tossing and turning, trying to figure out what was wrong with Paddy. I sat up with the realization, "He did it. He hit her. He kicked her or hit her with something. He went into a rage and he hurt her." I remembered seeing him kick Snoopy. Tim told me he had beaten Muggles. I had stopped him from hurting Bear. This was entirely possible. I began to believe that this was how it happened. I remembered Paddy's eagerness to leave Phil's house. She came immediately to the back of the car to be let in. She didn't want to say goodbye as she normally did. She wanted to leave, immediately.

I tried to set the idea aside, but it gnawed at me. I imagined Paddy being at Phil's house, day after day, while I was in Minnesota. I imagined Paddy being identified in his girlfriend's mind as "Jude's dog." She might have been annoyed to have this reminder of Phil's prior woman. Paddy might have exhibited old habits from when I lived there. Young Dancer had no such memories, and such a happy-go-lucky guy would have been delighted to be hanging out with "all the big dogs." Paddy was not happy-go-lucky. She was protective, guarded. She wouldn't understand another woman being in my bed.

Why did they lock Paddy in the family room? Why did Paddy, who had the strongest bladder of any of the dogs, pee in front of the door? Something happened with Paddy over Christmas. Something happened *to* Paddy.

I knew I would never get the true story from Phil. He knew better than to tell me that he or his girlfriend had hurt Paddy. I would never know. I could only imagine. Yet, somehow, I knew.

The next day I went again to visit Paddy. This time the vet told me all four of her legs were paralyzed. She lay in the crate with her head up but her four legs splayed out. I crawled in and joined her.

The vet opened the door on the crate, ducked and came in. He sat across from me. "She's not eating. She's not eliminating. She's given up," he said. "They do that sometimes."

He explained the options. We could take her to Albuquerque for an MRI and possibly learn more about what the problem was. The choice of treatment would be determined then. There were thousands of dollars associated with that option and no guarantees. Or, we could end it now by putting her to sleep. I could make the arrangements with them. I could be with her or not as I chose. He left, giving me time to think it over.

"Paddy, don't give up!" I pleaded, "I need you. Dancer needs you. Paddy, please stay with me." She looked at me with her big brown eyes. Of her entire beautiful body, all she could move was her head. She seemed to say that she would stay with me if she could. "Oh, Paddy, you have been such a good friend to me. I love you so much."

What could I do for her? The answer was not to put her on a stretcher, drive sixty miles to Albuquerque, and have them force her legs and torso around, trying to get a good position for an MRI. The vet wasn't even sure the MRI would give us the information we needed to heal her. He wasn't confident that she could be healed.

I believed she, too, was shattered by her lost illusion of Phil as a good master. Her master had beaten her, hurt her. What should I do? *She* seemed to have decided. She had given up, and honoring her decision was the only answer.

I petted her roughly; she loved it and gave her growl-purr. "Paddy, I have to let you go. I know you don't feel well. I know you don't understand what has happened to you. Paddy, I don't know how to make you better. I think this is what you want. I think you are ready to go. I guess you've done what I needed. I've started a new life. I'll be OK. You've given Dancer such a great start. But we will miss you so!

"I bet Bear will be glad to see you. He's been waiting for you." I ruffled her coat. "I bet you'll do your moan-howl on seeing him and he'll do his little coyote yips."

I heard myself say over and over, "I love you, Paddy. I pledge this to you. I pledge that your sacrifice is not for naught. I take on your strength. I accept your sacrifice in providing closure from a bad relationship. I emotionally disentangle myself from Phil. The veil is lifted. I will never again let illusion, denial, thoughts I want to be true color my seeing what is really happening."

From inside the crate with me, Dr. Pete again explained the procedure. I nodded with tears streaming down my cheeks. He administered the injection. Paddy went to sleep—and then she passed away.

I stayed with her for a while and petted her and thanked her for her friendship, her love and support. She had been my anchor and support in the year-and-a-half of my separation and divorce. She had been my best friend since Bear had died three-and-a-half years before. She, Bear and I had had several good years before that. All in all, I was with Paddy for nine years, from her puppyhood to final illness.

Bear and Paddy were bookends for my life with Phil. Bear at the start of my relationship with Phil and Paddy, signaling the complete emotional end with Phil. I will never be so fooled again by illusion.

I think I was given an extra month with Paddy to appreciate her some more and show her my love. She could have died in December while I was in Minnesota, but she didn't, and I had a wonderful month with her. I was so grateful for the "Paddy Day" we had shared only a week before.

When I left Paddy at the vet's, I wanted to be with Dancer, so I picked him up and I took him on the same walk Paddy and I had taken during our "Paddy Day." Although Paddy was pooped out after fifteen minutes, Dancer and I went farther and he did not get pooped out at all.

Dancer missed Paddy, too.

He continued to wait at the gate. I'm sure he was waiting for her to come back. In the house, he'd scratch on the spot on the floor in front of the television set where she used to lie. I would lay a towel down on the spot so he could lay on it. He went from room to room, plopping himself down—no, that's not right either, he seemed to think and he'd get up again and try another room. He would wake up in the middle of the night whining. I realized that this was the same time of night when he'd get up off his pillow and go join Paddy on hers. He liked to cuddle. I would call him over and pet him for a few minutes and then put Paddy's pillow on top of his. Then he would have a comfortable spot and her smell.

Paddy. My Perfect Paddy. I am grateful for the years we had together. She guarded me, loved me and made me laugh. She lost her pack because of me, yet there was no place she would rather have been than by my side. She helped me through my divorce, helped me build a new life. Paddy opened my eyes to things that I had wished to be true but were not. And thanks to Paddy, I will never again allow what I want to be true delude me. For that, too, I will always be grateful.

Thank you, Paddy, my dear friend. I believe you are with Bear now and that I will see you once again. I love you. Thank you for loving me.

Muggles, So Handsome

March 8, 2000 – August 6, 2013

Muggles always wanted to be my dog like Lil Bear was and eventually like Paddy was, but Muggles was Phil's dog. Even so, I was the one who fed him, groomed him, trained him and kept an eye on his health. For all ostensible purposes, he *was* my dog. At least he was for the first eight-and-a-half years of his life. I lost him in the divorce.

Muggles was my most beautiful dog. He was sable and gold. Strands of his fur were of more than one color. In some places his fur was dark at his skin, golden at the ends, and in others dark at the end and golden close to the skin. When my husband had him shaved for the New Mexico summer heat, Muggles had a different color pattern marked by a broad black stripe down his back, like an English saddle with a rump flap. It wasn't there when his hair was long. The skin along his backbone was loose enough that when he walked his fur shimmered. I loved to comb it. When people remarked on his beauty and asked us what breed of dog he was, we said, "Tibetan Mastiff," but really he was a black Lab–golden Chow-Chow mix.

Muggles wasn't always beautiful, though; he was an awkward young dog. Fat and roly-poly as a pup, he looked out of balance, with ears too large for his head. We called him "monkey dog."

Muggles came from a litter in the neighborhood. Phil, Tim and I, along with the dogs we had at the time: Lil Bear, Snoopy, and Sheltie, often took walks along the dirt country roads and acequias of Valencia County, New Mexico.

Our neighbor Richard's house and gardens were along the way, and we frequently stopped to talk with him and say hello to his black Lab, Lady. On one such walk, Richard invited us to see Lady's pups, which were about five weeks old at the time. They were all fat balls of fur, but the fattest and the furriest was lying under the old wringer style washing machine discarded in the yard. Phil said, "We want that one!" Later in the day he went back and put a tiny red collar on the puppy. We stopped by several times after that, eagerly waiting for the pups to turn eight weeks old. At last the time came, and Richard brought the little bundle of fur to the house. We were all sitting around the living room, watching the puppy poke around and get introduced to the other dogs and cats in the house. Phil was watching carefully. "That's not the one I picked out," he said. "Oh Phil," I thought with a sigh. His overly active imagination had misled him before. I was surprised to see Richard blush and turn pink under his dark skin. "Well, my ex-wife wanted that one," he said. "What could I do?"

"You can take this one back. Tell her that puppy has already been spoken for and give her this one." Phil opened the door for Richard and he left with the puppy in his arms.

I don't know how Richard did it, but two days later he returned with the correct puppy. "His name is Muggles," Phil said, and so he became.

Muggles always wanted to be wherever the action was. I had my dog, Lil Bear, and he went with me just about everywhere I went. When I went to our second home and my office, I always took Lil Bear with me. One evening when I loaded up the Subaru, six-month-old Muggles jumped in along with Bear. He scrunched as far back from the hatch door as possible so he couldn't be dragged out. But Phil didn't like his dog wanting to go with me. He reached in to pull him out. Muggles growled at him. This was serious misbehavior. "Leave," he said to me with his hand tightly on Muggles' collar. Soon thereafter Phil changed his mind about keeping Muggles "intact" and he was neutered. That was the only time Muggles misbehaved.

I don't remember Muggles and I having much one-on-one time. Sometimes he got to stay with me along with one or two of the other dogs. I never took a walk with just him and me. He was Phil's dog, and even if Phil didn't do those things with him, no one else could. But we had our time together in the evening as the family and pets gathered in the family room to watch television. That was when I combed Muggles and ran my hands through his fur as he lay on his side on the carpet. His fur was so soft and sweet smelling!

Muggles was a disciplined dog with a regular schedule. Every night he went to bed at 9:30 pm. When all the rest of us: humans, dogs, cats, were in the family room, he would lumber up from his spot, leave the room and lie down on the cool kitchen tiles to sleep. "It's 9:30," we'd say.

Once he was grown, he kept himself at eighty-nine svelte pounds. I always found that amazing.

Muggles did become a very well behaved dog. His discipline was tested one Saturday morning at my stepson Tim's football game. As the dog trainer of the family, I had decided to bring Muggles along for some socializing. He and I were along the fence, behind the cheering parents on the sidelines. A young boy, a toddler, ran up to put his arms around Muggles' neck. This meant his dirty diaper squished into Muggles nose. Muggles didn't growl this time, he just turned to me with a pitiful look in his eyes. "I have to take *this*?"

Then there's the time Muggles and Paddy saved Tim's life.

The three of us humans and the three dogs were coming back from a walk around the acequias. I had Bear on a leash to stop him from chasing the neighbors' dogs back and forth along the fence. We were almost home. We didn't know that Tom, a near neighbor, had gotten a new dog from the shelter—an untested, full grown German Shepherd. Young Tim was tired and lagging behind. As Tim walked past Tom's property, the dog came up behind him and gave him a chomp on the back of the leg. Tim screamed and fell to the ground.

In a flash, Muggles and Paddy raced back. Paddy smashed into the dog and rolled him away from Tim. She then stood her ground…over Tim. Muggles tore after the Shepherd and chased him until he was cornered against Tom's fence. He held him there until we released him. The pair of them, Muggles and Paddy, had worked together perfectly!

Tim's pant leg had taken the brunt of the German Shepherd's bite. When I examined him, there was no blood and no bite wounds. Still, he had been terrified, and I made Hero and Heroine cards for Tim to give to Muggles and Paddy for their bravery. It helped him deal with the fear he now felt toward dogs.

Unfortunately, human family harmony broke down eventually, and I lost access to Muggles when Phil and I divorced. It broke my heart to lose Muggles. There was much I left behind, and Muggles was the most precious.

I did see Muggles once after the divorce. Phil had been making money from selling classic car parts. He had half a dozen classic but rusted out Oldsmobile car shells still sitting on my property, long after he was due to haul them away. He asked to come up and take some chrome off one of the cars; he had a buyer he said. "I'll bring Muggles," he enticed.

When Muggles jumped out of the truck and raced over to me, I was delighted. We went to the far side of the property. Muggles and I walked for a bit and then sat on a slight hill, hip to hip, just glad to be together. I put my arm around him, his head as high as mine. It was wonderful to be with him. My beautiful Muggles. We were content.

Eventually Phil gave a shout, and our time was up. When we came around the house, I saw that Phil had loaded up much more than we had agreed upon. "He's going to give me Muggles in exchange!" I thought with glee. Paddy had died a few weeks earlier and I thought it possible that Phil would think of such a swap. Muggles walked at my side as I headed toward Phil. "Come on! In the car!" he yelled at Muggles. "In the car!" Instead of obediently jumping into the car, Muggles hid behind me. Not a swap, I realized.

"Let him stay with me—just for a few days. I'll bring him to you!" I begged and bargained. "You're taking much more than we agreed to. That's not fair! You owe me!"

"Yeah, tell it to the judge." He grabbed Muggles by the collar and dragged him to the car. "In!" They drove off.

"'Tell it to the judge'?" That was not a possibility. I was experienced with lawsuits by that time. Through the probate battle over Phil's mother's estate during which I, too, was sued for $180,000, I learned the difference between a lawyer and a really good lawyer. Really good lawyers are expensive. With that lesson, I hired a really good lawyer to represent me in my divorce from Phil. He still gained more of our community property than I received. As a result, I was deeply in debt to both probate and divorce lawyers, and I owed a significant amount of money to the IRS and the state. When Paddy had died the month before, I had put all her expenses on a credit card to be paid "some day." My goal with Phil was to wrench myself out of his grasp forever. I would not pay spousal support. I would not maintain contact with him. I would get out of this financial debt and build a new life for myself.

I couldn't force Phil to let Muggles stay with me for a few days, much less have him give Muggles to me. He had shown me in the past that any anger on my part would be met by his and it would rapidly escalate to a meanness and violence I could not match and did not want to. In fear for my safety, I had learned to be quiet. I had no voice. I could beg. I could plead. But those were strategies that had no effect on Phil. He had brought Muggles with him that day to distract me while he took more than we had agreed to. I watched Muggles as they drove away, my heart broken, once more. I did not see Muggles again.

It had been more important to me to be with Muggles for an hour, though, than to safeguard those junk car parts from Phil. I had gotten the better deal in the end. One last time, we had felt and exulted in the bond between us.

Three and a half years after I had last seen Muggles, I had a dream about him so real I thought it was actually happening. In the dream, I became aware of nestling my nose, my whole face into his furry side as he laid stretched out on the floor in front of me. He smelled good. I could feel his soft fur, the fur I used to brush and brush until it was silky and glowed. I felt again the love that flowed between us when we had had those moments in awakened life. I felt happy, so joyful to be with him. I sensed that Muggles felt happy, too; he was content. It was so pleasant. Then that feeling began to slip away. I came to realize that Muggles was dying. He had come to me to aid his passing, to make it safe. What a tribute, Muggles. What a beautiful way to say goodbye. Thank you.

My Muggles story closes with a conversation with Tim, my stepson, which I had soon after my Muggles dream. At the time of the divorce, for his own reasons, Tim had dissociated himself from his father, too. During the years since, we had been in occasional contact. Sometimes we went to the movies or had a weekend overnight at my house.

I called him, and Tim was glad to hear from me. With a bit of chagrin, however, he told me that he had resumed contact with his father. "You know how he always gets the ladies! I'm going to find out how he does it." I realized that male teen hormones had kicked in and that I was going to lose Tim, too. I could not maintain a relationship with him while he developed a close relationship with his father and modeled himself after him. I also did not want to keep that invisible but oh-too-real thread connecting me to his father.

Before we signed off, I wanted to know, "How is Muggles?"

"Muggles is dead."

"What happened to him?" I asked. Phil had taken Muggles up into the Jemez Mountains with him last winter. When it was time to leave, Phil said he hadn't been able to find Muggles so he had left without him.

I felt a hot surge of anger when I heard this. Muggles was thirteen at the time, an old dog. How was he going to manage in the wild New Mexico mountains? And in winter! I believed Phil had purposely left him; Phil didn't want to dig a hole for that big old dog! And he didn't want to pay a vet to put him down humanely. He had left Muggles in the mountains to die. I hung up the phone, saddened and angry.

"How odd that I had that dream about Muggles earlier this week," I thought. It seemed like he died then. Now I've come to believe that someone probably took Muggles in that winter and that Muggles was alive between the time Phil abandoned him and he came to me in that dream. I believe that Muggles did die while perceiving me to be with him. Now he is with Bear and Paddy.

The pack is back.

Dancer, Forever Young

October 28, 2008 – July 13, 2011

During the two short years we were together, I saw Dancer mature from an exuberant clown of a young fellow to the stalwart lynchpin of the family. His joy in life helped lead me out of the anger and resentment I had felt after my divorce, and his courage and staunch companionship helped me face the darkness of the steps I still had to take to disentangle myself financially from my ex-husband.

I adopted Dancer from the local shelter. Paddy, a senior dog at that time, and I picked him out. Leading "Floyd" as he was called at the shelter to the car, it appeared that this dog had never been socialized to humans. He must have been on the streets all of his young life. He certainly had never been in a car, and he did not want to get into one now. And he most definitely did not want to get into the plastic crate I had brought for him. He wriggled and danced his way back to the ground. Finally I scooped him into the car, pushed aside the crate, and double leashed him to clips on either side of the cargo area. Gingerly I drove home not knowing how this wild dog would respond to being tied or to the car's movement.

In those first few days as I got to know him, I came to realize that not only had he never been in a car, he didn't know how to be in a house. Jumping onto, or over, a couch was no different than jumping onto or over a boulder. Because of all of his energy and wriggly-ness, we named him "Dancer."

And a Dancer he was. When I took him to the vet for his wellness check, Dancer rolled and wiggled all over the floor. Not because he wanted to get away, but just because he wanted to play and was always on the move. The vet called him a clown. We decided he was eight-to-ten-months old, not a year. I declared his birthday to be October 28, the feast date of my patron saint, St. Jude, and also coinciding with the date I had left my marital home. I proclaimed Dancer part English Pointer, part Border Collie. The breeds fit his energy as well as his black and white dotted coloring.

On a day-to-day basis, his exuberance and energy wore out both Paddy and me. I had a large ten-foot by ten-foot outdoor dog run with an igloo kennel. At the end of each day, after dinner, we put him into the dog run and went into the house, exhausted. That first month he spent the night outside.

His exile to the outdoors ended on the Fourth of July. A dog that is not scared of fireworks is definitely preferable to one that is. Paddy was not scared. I wanted her help in ensuring that Dancer would not be scared either.

On the third of July, as it got dark, I heard fireworks going off at a distance. Soon my neighbors joined in, shooting off elaborate fireworks that went off nearby, some even exploding overhead. From our comfortable spot in the house, I called out across the living room to Paddy, "Let's get Dancer!" and out we went to rescue him. As I approached the kennel, however, I realized I did not want him to get the sense that he had to be rescued and that fireworks were something to be afraid of. I slowed down and grabbed a small lawn chair. Paddy and I went into the dog run with Dancer. He was glad to see us but not nervous. The three of us stayed in the enclosure for almost an hour. I oohed and aahed over the fireworks to indicate they were things of pleasure while Paddy demonstrated calmness.

Then the three of us went inside. I situated Dancer on the dog pillow that was waiting for him next to Paddy's. I put a leash on him and tied it to the bedpost to make sure he didn't wander through the house that night, and from then on he slept indoors. That marked the end of Dancer's initiation; he had become a full-fledged member of the family. He was the youngster a pack needs to train and nurture. Once again, Paddy had a pack. With Tigger, the gray, blue-eyed feline of the household, our family was complete. Little did we know that Dancer would become the glue that held our entire family together.

Paddy was trained to behave with cats but she never got friendly with them like Bear had with Pumpkin. So, Tigger immediately put his hopes on Dancer. I never understood if Dancer liked Tigger, but Tigger liked Dancer! No sooner would Dancer get curled up on his dog pillow than Tigger would join him, cuddling close. I don't know if Dancer was embarrassed or if he liked it, but he did put up with it. The two of them curled up on a pillow became a familiar household sight.

Whenever I described my new dog to others, my first word was "exuberant." If there was no one to play with, chase or attack, he found his own games. Sometimes he picked up a large stick and just ran with it. I have a picture of him with a stick twice as long as himself. He's running so fast his ears are flopping up and behind him. Other times, I put an old soccer ball out for him to play with. He would kick it with his front feet and race across the lot. I called him, "Dancer, the Soccer Playing Dog." He loved to have me watch him, clap and encourage him. If the ball got out of sight, he picked it up in his mouth and brought it back to the imaginary central viewing area in front of me.

There was an old flatbed car trailer on the edge of the lot. It was one of the items Phil had left behind. Sometimes Paddy, Dancer and I sat on it to watch the sunset. I also used it to train Dancer to jump up and off on command. When he jumped off, he did not just jump down. For the sheer enjoyment of it, he jumped straight out, adding more seconds in flight and several feet to his jump.

One time he had me laughing so hard that tears were cascading down my cheeks. This was a day we had left Paddy at home and had gone on an excursion in the car. This would be practice for him being in the car for a longer period of time, and for him to learn not to eat the upholstery.

I drove up to the Parajito Mountain ski hill. It was open for the season but closed that day. Dancer was quite taken by the sight of all the Ponderosa pines as we climbed the twisty road. I opened the back window an inch or two. The air was brisk; the pine smell of the trees was strong. Dancer whined with excitement.

I parked the car and we walked from the parking lot into an area where roads into the woods had been plowed and were snow packed. There were lots of aspens along with the tall pines; it was truly beautiful. Along the side of the road, the snow was deep and in drifts. I noted a picnic area off to the side with a picnic table buried in snow up to its table top.

I had Dancer on a six-foot leash. We went uphill on one of the snow packed roads. In his eagerness, he was pulling hard on the leash. Walking at 10,000 feet of elevation, I was just as glad to have his pull to help propel me along. Nevertheless, after a bit, I had to stop to catch my breath. Dancer was getting bored waiting for me; he was ready to go-go-go!

So, I took him off the leash. Dancer then proceeded to gallop up the road and back to me—he must have traveled a mile for every block I walked! Soon this was not enough for him, and he went "off road." He bounded into the drifts along the side of the road, jumping like a rabbit through snow higher than his belly. He sank deep and jumped again, grabbing snow in his mouth and flinging it over his back. He was delirious with joy! I, however, was slowly putting one foot in front of the other, breathing heavily. I encouraged him to run first in one direction, back to me, and then out in another direction. After he had run in all four directions, each time back to me, I had caught my breath enough to continue up the hill. After awhile, I had had enough and decided it was time to turn back. Surely Dancer, too, was tired out. But no, his exuberant young self ran down hill and back up to me with as much energy and joyfulness as he had at our start. Even on the drive down the mountain, he was wide eyed, looking at all the trees, eyes intently on the road through the two front seats. Only after we reached the busy streets of Santa Fe did he yield to exhaustion and fall asleep, his head hanging over the edge of the back seat where he had last been trying to keep his eyes on the road.

Ever after, Dancer was eager to go for a ride in the car, hoping, I believe, to duplicate that tremendous day among the aspens and pines of Parajito Mountain. Thereafter, I had to be careful opening the hatchback so the door did not hit him as he jumped in even before the hatch was fully open.

There are so many more stories to tell about Dancer! He always wanted to be up high. He would jump onto the top of the old junk cars left in my yard by Phil, soon to be my "ex." The cars bordered my neighbors' privacy fence. Later I heard my neighbor Frank's story: "I was working in the yard and I felt eyes on me. I looked all around and then I looked up higher. There was a black and white dog perched at the height of the fence, watching me." He came to be called "Peeping Dancer" and was the entree to friendship with neighbors behind a fence too high and dense to communicate through easily. Eventually the junk cars left the property and I built a "doggie jungle gym" out of straw bales to amuse Dancer in his job of watching the entire neighborhood.

Sometimes I took Dancer and Paddy to the dog park. I felt that Dancer needed some dog-socializing. Paddy, however, didn't appreciate a dog park; she had plenty of room to run at home. But she would dutifully follow two feet behind me as I walked the park. Dancer, on the other hand, thought it was a wonderful concept. He ran ahead of us. I believe he took liberties because he knew he had Paddy, the Rottweiler, to back him up. I remember one day in particular, when he crashed a party of two German Shepherd Dogs. They weren't too sure about this obnoxiously playful fellow, but when his "mama" came around the corner to see what he was up to, there was no issue of complaints.

Dancer also proved to be a good friend. The night I learned my divorce was final, I felt great anguish. I had yearned for a life partner and had spent years looking for that person. I thought I had found him. With that understanding I had devoted ten years of physical, emotional and financial resources into making the relationship work and to ensure a pleasant retirement for my husband and me. Now all that was lost. I felt beaten, used up and depleted of resources. I sobbed that night as if my heart was broken, and indeed it was. Paddy and Dancer stayed close. That next morning was when I realized I had lost the hearing in my right ear.

Paddy taught Dancer a number of things as well as not being afraid of fireworks and other loud noises. She taught him to sit patiently while his dinner was being prepared; she taught him to ride calmly in the back of the car; and, following the long line of dogs going back to Bear's mentor, Arrow, she taught him to hunt lizards, the wiry and fast desert salamanders that populated my lot. And Dancer loved Paddy. He took in everything she taught him. In addition to being his mentor and the alpha dog of the pack, I believed Paddy fulfilled a mother dog role that he little experienced during his young life on the streets.

I've written elsewhere about how devastating Paddy's death was. She suddenly and inexplicably lost the use of her legs and I had her euthanized. Pertinent here is how devastating it was to Dancer.

When Paddy collapsed, my only focus was to get her to the vet. Before I drove away, I shoved Dancer into the outdoor kennel. He never saw her again. He never knew what happened to her. When Bear died, all the other dogs were there, and they knew he had died. They may have been forlorn, but they were not puzzled. I don't think Dancer ever stopped looking for Paddy. For months after Paddy's death, when I returned home he would come not to the driver's door but would wait around back for me to lift the cargo door and reveal Paddy. Other times I saw him standing at the gate looking off into the distance.

If I had the chance to do it over, I would have brought Dancer with me to the vet, and he and I would have been with Paddy when she went to sleep for the last time. As weird as it sounds, I believe he would have been more at peace if he'd understood what had happened. As it was, my thoughts were not about him at all. In my grief over Paddy, I shut him out.

Dancer was a small dog, about forty-five pounds. I didn't think he could handle guard dog duty in our remote country location. So, I began again to look for a Rottador, like Paddy, to complement our pack. After a search at the animal shelter, Dancer and I brought home eight-week-old Dixie, the boldest of a litter of Rottweiler-Labradors.

After Paddy's death, and with the addition of a puppy to the household, Dancer quickly matured. He took his role as Dixie's mentor seriously and passed on the training from dog to dog going back to Bear and Arrow. He became more alert, watchful. Was he continuing his watch for Paddy's return, or was he following in her footsteps and serving as watch dog?

A few months after Paddy's death, Dancer began digging under the fence. He became an escape artist. I'm sure he was looking for Paddy. The first time Dancer escaped was one day I was not there, and it was the most dramatic. Four-month-old Dixie was not to be left behind. The pair traveled miles before they finally sprawled exhausted on the shaded tile of a young couple's portal four miles from my house. I was in Albuquerque when I got the call, "I have your dogs." I thought it was a ransom call! Dancer never went that far again, but he continued to dig under the fence frequently. I believe he may also have had some Basset Hound in him. Once I timed him—three minutes from the back door, a fresh dig under the fence, and on the other side! So, I had the entire three-acre lot retrenched to put wire mesh six to eight inches into the ground.

A few more stories from this time with Dancer: I was struggling to clear up the last loose ends of my spiteful divorce. Phil had been granted the homestead we had totally remodeled during our marriage. He chose to not make payments on the house, and he did not clear my name from ownership. As foreclosure loomed, he abandoned the house, totally stripping it of any items of value. He took all the appliances, the toilets, water heater, furnace—even the ceiling vigas and the external doors to the house and garage, as well as all the protective fencing around the lot. When I learned about this, I realized that to protect myself from local government legal action, I had to take responsibility for cleaning up and boarding up the house. By that time, the property had been open to the elements for an unknown period of time. Dancer was my companion to enter that filthy, dark building. He was willing to face skunk or squatter. He came with me on every subsequent trip until the property was clean and boarded up.

Still, with playful Dancer, there were moments of great joy during this time. One special time was mornings. Once I stirred in bed, it was Dancer who encouraged me to get up—"It's a new day!" he seemed to say. Since the animals were not allowed on my bed, he did this by keeping one back leg on the floor, and stretching every other inch of his body until he reached his nose to my neck just under the ear lobe. "Good morning! Get up!" he seemed to say. And once I was up, I in turn, sang a silly good morning song to the dogs that was a happy remnant from my childhood; it went, "Good morning! Good morning! K. E. Double L. O. Double Good—Kellogg's best to you!"

Dancer also saw me into bed every night. He lay on the rug next to my bed until I fell asleep. Then he moved to the living room putting him between the front door and the rest of us. Dancer, now two-and-a-half, was coming into his own as a mature, confident dog.

Such was life in the household that now consisted of Dancer, Dixie, Tigger and me.

This part of the story starts with the great wildfire of June, 2011. The "Las Conchas fire," at that time the largest fire to ever take place in New Mexico, reached 30,000 feet into the air, so large that it created its own weather—airplanes would fly around it rather than get caught in its downdrafts. On the ground, the wildfire had a front 500 feet high and it moved faster than one acre per second. I heard from others that the sound of the fire was louder than a locomotive going through your bedroom. This fire required the evacuation of Los Alamos National Laboratory and the entire town of Los Alamos. It eventually devastated 150,000 New Mexico acres.

It was a Sunday evening and I had just said goodbye to friends who had come to visit me and each other. One couple was from the East Coast, one from the West. We had had a great few days savoring Santa Fe life and green chile. I was returning home, driving south on the two-lane, paved county road headed back to my house. Earlier we had noticed a spiral of smoke in the mountains; wildfires had become so common in New Mexico that we did not pay much attention. But now, as I turned west down the road toward my house, the fire looked close. The sky was a wall of red before me. "Where is the fire?! Where is it?" It looked so close, I was positive it had reached my house another mile up the road.

I maneuvered curve after curve of this county road, driving faster and faster. As I drove I became more positive that the fire had reached my house. "Oh my God! I don't care about the house! I left the dogs locked in the outdoor kennel! Dancer and Dixie. There is nothing they can do. I locked my dogs in and they are going to burn to death in this massive wildfire!" My foot pressed harder on the pedal.

I skidded into the turn to my road—Paseo de Angel—the way of the angels. "Please dear God. Please. Not my dogs!" I learned later that the wall of fire was 500 feet high. I do not know how to judge the closeness of a fire of that height. That is as tall as a fifty-story building. We do not have buildings that tall in New Mexico. I learned later that it was moving at thirty miles an hour. As the crow files, the fire was less than thirty miles away. Was it headed in my direction? I could not tell. The entire western sky was aflame.

The car stumbled to a stop in front of the gate to my house. I slumped forward in emotional exhaustion. "All right. The fire is not here. It is not here! OK. What am I going to do? The dogs are safe. The fire is not here, yet. What am I going to do?"

I left the gate open and came to a stop in front of the house. A plan was beginning to form in my mind. I first went to the outdoor kennel. Dancer and Dixie, trained to trust natural phenomenon, were not afraid of a little ole wildfire. They happily greeted me and expected their dinner. Nevertheless, once I opened the kennel door, I fell to my knees and took them in my arms. "Oh, my darling-darlings."

A plan materialized. "If I need to go north, I will go to Colorado Springs. Sherry will take me in. If I need to go south, I will go to Albuquerque. Surely this fire will not be allowed to devastate Albuquerque! Diane will take me and the dogs in. However, I will stay here with bags packed until I am sure what direction the fire is headed."

I went into the house. I packed a bag. I took my important papers, and my silver concha belts. Funny how the mind crystallizes at a moment like this. No pictures; not even my precious journals, I am sorry to say. Money. A few days' clothing. Some food and water. That's what counted. Whatever burns, burns. I gathered dog food bowls, water, dog food, protein bars for me. My suitcase went into the front seat. What to do about the cat? Dixie would eat him if they shared space. I remembered the plastic crate. That's where I would put Tigger. I left the Subaru facing the street, the gate open and the keys in the ignition. The back was for the dogs and Tigger and their things. I had the front seats. We were ready to go.

All night Dancer and I watched the red sky and tried to judge how close the fire was. I sat in the outdoor glider with Dancer at my knee. Dixie slept. Finally, it was almost daylight; it was clear the fire had shifted to the north, along the forest ridge, not toward La Cienega and my home. I brought the dogs inside and we went to bed.

This next part of the story is not as easy to relay as the sweet reminiscences above—of Dancer, the exuberant clown, Dancer so soft and cuddly, Dancer gamboling in the snow drifts of the ski hill, Dancer who walked with me into the depths of the stripped and abandoned house, unafraid, confident we could deal with whatever we found. Dancer, who bravely stared down the largest wildfire of New Mexico history.

In the morning after our night watching the Las Conchas fire, Dancer, as was usual, had moved from his spot next to my bed to the dog pillow in the front room. Dixie was in her crate in the bedroom so she wouldn't attack the cat. After I let the dogs out, I turned back into the living room, and I saw a puddle of water on the floor. "Did Dancer pee?" How unusual this was. "Was he scared by the fire?" I wondered. I wiped up the puddle and we continued through the day. I left my suitcase and the dogs' things in the car even though the fire seemed to be moving north and away from us.

Later in the day, I again noticed a puddle on the floor that seemed to be able to come only from Dancer. "He must have a urinary infection," I thought. Two more times I came across puddles. I made a vet appointment for the next day.

I was not very concerned during our visit at the vet's office. I believed that I would leave with antibiotics that would knock out a pesky urinary tract infection. We saw the vet. "I'm going to take some blood tests." Dancer and I waited in the exam room. I jiggled his leash; he waited patiently. She came back. "Dancer has diabetes."

"What?!" Dancer was a young, lean male. I had followed the vet's pre-scription of keeping him thin. Dancer did NOT fit the profile for diabetes—older, female and overweight. "This cannot be! I do not understand! I don't know anything about diabetes, but I know it is a serious disease. What does this mean? For Dancer? For me?"

I went home stunned. My world had changed. My young, healthy watch dog and companion was terribly sick. I began the routine of insulin shots twice daily, twelve hours apart. "You can deviate by half an hour on either side of the shot time." I took Dancer and the insulin in a refrigerator bag if I was going out at the dinner hour. I put an old shower curtain in the back of the car with copious towels on top to catch any urine if we traveled for more than half an hour. If at a friend's house it was: "No, Dancer has to stay outside, but put this in the refrigerator."

Dancer didn't get better. I went back to the vet twice for review of my shot giving technique and further training. I brought Dancer in every few days for further blood work. "It may take us a few weeks or a few months to get the right type and amount of insulin for his condition. His case is very unusual. I haven't seen anything like it in the hundreds of cases we've dealt with."

He drank huge amounts of water. I timed him. He drank for ninety sec-onds straight, then looked up at me, and went back to drink some more. He peed copious amounts every thirty to forty-five minutes. He could be in the house for only short periods of time. I remember one of the last times. He had just peed outside. I brought him in and he lay next to me on the floor as I lay on the couch. I dangled my arm to stay in constant physical contact with him. We napped peacefully for thirty minutes or so. Then it was time for him to go back outside.

Dixie and I spent much of our time outside with him. Dancer would lie in the shade, with one thump of his tail letting us know our company was welcome. Once again, Dancer spent his nights in the outdoor kennel. He had been with me for exactly two years.

Dancer lost his energy and his liveliness, and Dixie lost her playmate. He rarely responded to her attempts to wrestle, chase lizards or pull on a stick. Sometimes they walked the perimeter of the lot; now she was in front and he trailed behind. Only when he was needed as watch dog could he muster any strength. If Dixie called him, he would rush to the back fence to let the neighbor Pit Bull know he was still on the job.

Another time he over-exerted himself. I opened the front door to check on him. He stumbled up the three steps to the door and collapsed before he was through the threshold. He lay on the sheet I had put by the door for "accidents." I pulled the sheet forward so that he was totally in the house and I closed the door on the July sun. He didn't move. Tigger came over and cuddled next to him. I thought that was the end.

I had long ago run out of money. Vet bills were going on a credit card, to be paid, "someday."

On the Fourth of July, Dancer and I sat in the back of the Subaru with the tailgate wide open, me dangling my feet over the edge, Dancer's head on my lap. I heard him tell me as clearly as if he could speak, "Put me at peace." I didn't. It had only been a week since I had heard, "Dancer has diabetes." Surely something would change for the better. Instead he continued to go downhill rapidly.

Even though I was now feeding Dancer twice as much as before, in two weeks he had lost more than twenty percent of his body weight. He went from fifty to thirty-eight pounds. The disease was eating him up from the inside. I learned that diabetes can devour internal organs like the pancreas and kidneys. His fur was no longer soft, but dry and raspy.

The second week passed. When I pinched his skin for yet another shot, he commanded me: "Stop torturing me!"

Finally, I listened.

That last night Dixie and I stayed up as late as our eyes could manage. We stayed outside with him. Dancer was lethargic but happy to be with us. How did this happen so fast? I raged. It had been just two weeks since I'd learned he had diabetes. Just two weeks ago we had stayed up late into the night staring down the Las Conchas fire. "Oh my buddy, I am going to miss you so!"

When the time came, I took him for a last ride. Near the house was a beautiful oasis with large cottonwood trees and a small pond with a fountain. Dancer and I sat next to the pond. It had been two weeks and one day since we had learned he was ill. "Come, Dancer, it is time to go."

I loved Dancer. He was a great companion. In his eagerness to go places and experience anything, he was a better companion dog than Dixie ever was. He was more agreeable even than Paddy, who went, was well behaved but who would really have preferred to be home. He actually rivaled Bear as a companion dog (Bear, however, was better behaved when we got there).

The life lesson Dancer forced me to learn was to consciously decide, yes, I love my dog, but it is possible to "love" him too much. He's telling me he's done. Can I put my feelings aside and let him go?

In my childhood, I had absorbed the "cowboy code": Take care of your horse and he will take care of you. Feed and bed down the animals first, then yourself. When your animal is in pain and cannot recover, it is your responsibility to quickly and humanely end his life.

I would be lying if I said I wanted to devote the next ten years of my life to giving Dancer shots twice a day and incurring all the expense and effort required to manage his diabetes. Early in his diagnosis, I knew I could not maintain a life where I gave my dog a shot twice a day, evenly spaced at twelve hours apart. I spoke with friends who had made that choice with their elderly Lab, therefore keeping her with them an additional two years. Even with two of them their life was quite curtailed. Someone had to be home every twelve hours. "We wouldn't do it again, Jude. Don't do it."

I had to travel for my work. The kennel did not have people on premises at the required twelve-hour intervals. My neighbor, potential pet sitter, said no she couldn't do shots. She could not even be a backup for me when I was home. In the back of my mind, I knew I could not sustain this schedule, or the emotional rollercoaster involved with Dancer's highs and lows. Dancer made it easier for me by not responding to treatment.

I wonder now if Dancer had diabetes insipidus, a totally different type of diabetes than he was treated for, one also with symptoms of excessive thirst and copious urination. It is rare, and genetically transmitted. It most frequently occurs in young male dogs and is not treated by insulin. Otherwise, his lack of response to treatment is puzzling. I wonder sometimes if he had made up his mind to go find Paddy. He had trained Dixie for a year and a half. She was as old as he was when Paddy left. Perhaps he felt his job was done and that he had left me adequately cared for.

I thank you, Dancer, for the two years we spent together. My playful, clown dog, who so exuberantly cheered me up during the depths of my painful divorce. Who matured into a confident watch dog, training Dixie in her duties as next dog of the house. Dancer, proud, dignified and true. May the good Lord be with you. May sunshine and happiness surround you. In my heart you'll always stay…forever young. For-ever young.

Dixie, Neighborhood Watch Dog

January 1, 2010 – unknown

When I came to, my cheek was in dirt. I was lying on my stomach, outside. I could see my house in the distance. I could see out of my right eye; my left eye was pressed into the dirt and rock embankment. I felt a weight on the small of my back. Dixie was lying as close to me as she could; her chin and neck lay across the small of my back.

That was when everything changed for Dixie and me. But let me begin earlier.

◇◇◇◇◇◇◇◇◇◇◇◇◇◇◇◇◇◇◇◇◇◇◇◇

Not too long after Paddy died, I decided I needed a guard dog. My divorce was quite bitter; Phil was proving to be unpredictable and did not keep his promises. Dancer was a wonderful companion, but I needed a dog like Paddy had been.

One experience with Phil settled the idea. I was outside picking up dog doo-doo. Head down, I was processing the insights I had learned from Paddy's death. I was positive Phil had beaten her when she stayed with him during the Christmas holidays and that that had led to her paralysis and death.

Lost in thought, I was walking along, eyes alert for fresh brown or old graying dog doo-doo, wearing my hospital gloves and carrying a plastic grocery bag. I leaned down, plopped a specimen into the bag, then did it again, and again. Eyes down, thinking about what I believed Phil had done to Paddy, I had the sudden realization, "I'm scared of him. I don't trust him to not hurt me, either." As I had that thought, I looked up and saw that at that very moment Phil was climbing over the padlocked gate into my yard. I was horrified and felt panicked.

I called upon the strength I promised Paddy I would have and I pulled myself together. "Phil! Don't climb over my fence! You are supposed to call before you come here."

"I just want to talk," he wheedled, but I refused to talk with him and he left.

Later that day while looking online, I was surprised when a litter of Rottweiler-Labradors showed up on the Santa Fe Animal Shelter adoption site. They had come in that morning. Dancer and I were first in line the following day, a Sunday. I picked the females out of the litter and spent time with two—a red one and a black one. I brought the black female out to Dancer to examine. With his approval, I signed the paperwork and we brought "Dixie" home.

It was winter, and an eight-week old puppy needs to go outside during the middle of the night. I had donned my old but warm full-length down coat the first three nights but thereafter I left it up to Dancer. I opened the front door, scooted Dixie out and said to Dancer, "You take her." Ah! The benefits of having an older dog to help with training! They are tremendous.

Dancer brought Dixie back inside, and we settled into our respective beds. Before long, however, Dixie joined Dancer on his dog pillow and cuddled up next to him.

Dixie was sweet at night, but during the day—what a hellion! One afternoon I found Dancer with Dixie's whole head in his mouth. It was the only way he found to stop her from nipping at him, pulling on his ears, in all ways being a constant pest. Another time, they were playing tug of war, a favorite game of theirs. Dixie got so frustrated at not being able to win that she growled sharply at Dancer. Dancer, pulling on his end of the rope, looked over at me as if to say, "What have we gotten into?" At six months old, she was fifty pounds and with her long legs already larger than Dancer.

I treasured every moment with those dogs. Mornings in particular were our time. The morning routine started with Dancer waking me. Then I opened the door of Dixie's crate by the side of my bed. She rolled over in anticipation of my fingers walking across the carpet, and I scratched her tummy. I let the dogs out, fed and closed the cat in the laundry room, made a cup of pour-over drip coffee for myself and took it outside to walk the perimeter of the large lot with the dogs. The smells of juniper and the sight of a northern New Mexico sunrise made a beautiful start to the day.

Dixie loved Dancer and followed him constantly. If he went under the fence, she tried, too. She was only able to do that until she was about six months old. Then she was too big. She got in trouble a couple of times when she followed Dancer under the shed after rabbits. I found Dixie caught with just her head under the shed unable to loosen herself. I learned later from the handyman that Dancer had preceded her. Dancer, however, was able to get totally under the shed, turn around and then crawl out. Learning this made me wonder what kind of trouble these two were getting into that I didn't know about. So I took away the freedom that Paddy and Dancer had had to roam the lot freely when I was gone from home. Whenever I left, Dancer and Dixie went into the outdoor kennel.

At around five months of age, Dixie developed a huge abscess under her neck. I think she had swallowed a salamander when she and Dancer were hunting through the dry grasses. The vet thought it was a bee. During a six-week period, it required two surgeries and numerous additional pre- and post-surgery trips to the vet. Several of these visits required an overnight stay. By the end of that time, she had very strong car sickness and hated to get in the car. Besides not wanting to get in the car and her size and strength making it difficult to force her, her motion sickness symptoms were intense. Her drooling started immediately upon entering the car. Within ten minutes, she would vomit. One time, poor Dancer got it from both of Dixie's ends.

I have always prided myself on the care and attention I have given to dog obedience training. Dixie, however, was the exception. I stopped her Novice class when she was six months old because of the abscess and the surgical wound at her neck. Thereafter her car sickness made it very difficult to bring her to the dog training center I normally used for training and socialization. So she never had the training my other dogs have had. I knew I needed to work with her more.

I wrote in my journal,

She's got the sit-stay-come commands and pre-meal time behavior down well. Very good. But she needs lots more time on a leash. Twice in the last week she's hurt my hand. If Dixie could take the car better I could bring her to formal classes.

I worked and worked on her car sickness. We sat in the car with the hatch door open. I fed her in the car. We made short forays around the driveway. We went for longer drives. Nothing worked. Eventually I occasionally resorted to drugs the vet prescribed for her.

Dixie never acclimated to the cat. Poor Tigger wanted to be friends with her. Dixie, however, wanted to eat him. So, we began a continual program of one in/one out. Dixie outside, Tigger loose in the house. Dixie loose in the house, Tigger locked up in the laundry room. Dixie locked in her crate, Tigger loose in the house. Dixie wanted to know where the cat was, and she liked to watch him. Occasionally, when she was loose in the house, she would go into her crate. She wanted me to close the door of her crate and let the cat out. If I did, she stared at him, following his every movement.

During this time, I was feeling the financial effects of my business having gone cold. At the same time, my expenses related to the divorce and disentanglement from Phil skyrocketed. My divorce lawyer had kindly worked with me on credit. Because of my hotly contested divorce, I was in debt to her to the tune of $30,000. The state taxation people were not happy with me either. I owed them $20,000 in income and sales tax. The IRS sent me a letter of intent to seize my property for taxes owed.

As if that was not enough, my already impaired hearing was declining. After tests confirming this, my audiologist referred me to a highly regarded ENT doctor. He feared that I had acoustic neuroma. This is a brain tumor and would account for the sudden hearing loss I had experienced the summer prior. (A brain MTI showed that this was not the case. However, I did have a very nervous few weeks.)

Meanwhile, the dogs were digging out of the fence every chance they had. The rabbits in the field next to the fence were their target. Now I had to leave them in the outdoor kennel whenever I was not outside to keep an eye on them.

Finally, my business started to pick up. My clients were requesting my presence in several different cities nationwide. I desperately needed the money this work would provide me, so I grabbed every revenue-producing business trip I could.

This required leaving Dancer and Dixie at home. A few months prior, I had found the perfect pet sitter. Jessie was a vet tech at the animal hospital I took my dogs to. The hospital was only ten minutes from my house. Jessie agreed that she would come let the dogs out on her lunch break and by staying overnight each night she would let them out for a significant time in the evening and for thirty to forty-five minutes each morning before she went to work. This seemed the ideal situation, better than leaving the dogs in a commercial kennel. Dixie, after her stays at the vet, had come to hate being kenneled.

After a few out-of-town trips, however, I had serious doubts about my pet sitter. In October when I came home from a business trip so excited to be home and see Dancer and Dixie, I found the outdoor kennel filled with feces and their food bowls stuck on top. I was outraged. Jessica was to be here every morning, noon and evening to let them out. She had said she would spend nights here and that the dogs would be in the house. The dogs hated to eliminate in the kennel. They would only do this if there was absolutely no alternative. It appeared to me that they had not been let out of the kennel since I had left, five days before. I fired Jessica and struggled to find a new care plan.

As I described earlier, when Dixie was a year and a half old, Dancer had suffered from a rare type of canine diabetes that attacked young, trim, male dogs. After much soul searching and clear requests from Dancer, I put him down. Dixie and I were inconsolable, and in our sadness, we bonded tightly.

Dixie matured quickly without Dancer to rely on for guidance. Space by my side opened up and she claimed it. Many a time, we sat on the deck, me in my wrought iron chair, Dixie lying at my feet. I watched the ravens in the cottonwood tree. Dixie watched the shed for any indication of her target rabbit. She had become my loving companion and the watch dog I needed. Now we were Dixie, Tigger and me. And so we went into the fall and into the winter.

Dixie became a hero on one Saturday night. I was asleep. I don't know how long she was barking and growling before she got my attention. I was probably sleeping on my good ear and not hearing much. When I did hear her, my first thought was that the cat was too close to her crate. Then I realized other dogs were barking, and I thought they were in a call and refrain. Finally, I got it. This was not normal Dixie behavior. Something was wrong.

I looked out the bedroom windows. I couldn't see or hear anything. I let Dixie out the front door. She was nervous but barking ferociously. She ran down the deck steps, barked-barked-barked toward the shed, and then ran back up the steps, looking to me for approval and support. She ran to the shed again and then into the darkness behind it. The phone rang. It was my nearest neighbors.

Frank and Linda told me that three teenage boys were in my yard and trying to climb the fence into their yard. Dixie's barking had alerted them. They had called the sheriff, and when the sheriff arrived, we did the whole thing—looked for footprints, saw that my back fence was mangled behind the shed where the boys had scrambled over as fast as they could as Dixie chased them. Everyone, the Sheriff, neighbors, me, were pleased with Dixie and praised and petted her exuberantly. Dixie had come through. It was a growing up moment for her.

Thereafter, Dixie became quite the neighborhood watch dog. She loved the praise she had gotten for her intruder alert. She began keeping an eye on everything and would check with me to be sure I knew it. Various neighbors began to say things like, "Tell Dixie we're going camping for the weekend. Ask her to keep an eye on our place, too."

"My mom is ill; we have to leave. My cousin will be here morning and night to feed the horses. Otherwise, no one should be here. Tell Dixie." I dutifully relayed their requests.

Dixie had been eyeing a particular rabbit for months. He lived under the shed. One night she caught him. It was about ten at night. Although there was just a half moon, it was bright. I was out walking, enjoying the stars and moon shadows. At one point, Dixie raced past me chasing the rabbit. Quite awhile went by, then they came racing back. Dixie got between the rabbit and the shed. Just like a cowpony with an ornery steer, she darted first one direction, then the other and wouldn't let the rabbit dash under the shed for safety. Then, with a little squeal and a gulp, she had it.

"No! Dixie! No!!"

Of course my cries were to no avail. She had been stubbornly, persistently, diligently stalking that rabbit since…well, the previous June when she got stuck under the shed looking for it. The previous winter she'd been tracking it. She wasn't about to stop or to give it up now. She ran off with the rabbit and I went to bed. At midnight she barked and I let her in.

She was stiff in the morning, and I was sure her tummy didn't feel too good either. I got the rabbit head from her and dumped it in the garbage. I was able to check her poop. So far, so good.

Dixie was regularly plagued with muscle and joint injuries. Perhaps she grew too fast. A friend of mine, a longtime owner of Great Danes, said that you had to watch how fast the puppies grow and take them off puppy food sooner than for smaller breeds. And at twenty-nine inches tall at the shoulder, Dixie rivaled the size of a Great Dane. At ninety svelte pounds, she was lean, lanky and well muscled. She was fast enough to catch a rabbit, which she now did at least once a month.

In addition, post-Dancer, she had severe separation anxiety. At home she was OK if left outside in the kennel. Indeed, she was glad to go into the kennel. "Kennel up!" and she would trot in front of me with her rawhide bone in her mouth. When I returned, she picked up her bone again to show me she still had it.

But I couldn't leave her in the house. I did one time. She was recovering from yet another injury; it was cold outside and I didn't feel comfortable leaving her out. I left her in the bedroom with her rawhide bone. When I pulled through the driveway and up to the bedroom window, I saw Dixie's face in the middle of the window, holding the bone in her mouth. It took me a moment to realize that she had shredded the wood blinds and was staring at me through the hole she had made. Another time, she got out of her in-house crate; I found scratch marks on every outside door in the house and furniture was knocked over in her scramble back and forth across the house to get out.

I came up with a new solution for Dixie care while I traveled. A friend of mine had just lost her dog and was amenable to watching mine. With my new business revenue, I was able to pay her for her time. Dixie seemed to settle down. By the fall of 2012, I had her in a stable state. She was on glucosamine, metacam and periodic acupuncture treatments.

Dixie turned three as we entered 2013. She was beautiful with her glossy black coat and tall, confident stature. And fast! I loved to watch her run. We had our special quiet moments, too. These were often outside, generally on the outdoor loveseat where she could jump up and sit next to me. She would sprawl out, taking up most of the seating area, leaving me just enough to be comfortable. She liked to put her head on my thigh and have me pet her as I talked on the phone or gazed in reverie at the distant mountains. I had given up on the Tigger-Dixie wars and had brought Tigger to my sister Bernie's house where I knew he would be loved. Dixie and I were happy, relaxed.

Within three months, our brief respite of my financial stability and her good health both came to an abrupt halt. My major client cancelled their contract. A week later Dixie took a fall on ice while careening around a corner of the house in answer to my call for her.

The vet said this was the big one that he had predicted would happen. A year ago we had done baseline X-rays. Dr. Pete had noted the unstable position of her knee bones then. Although she had long been plagued with muscle and joint injuries, they had not been as serious as this. This was bone on bone in her right rear leg. She was a stoic dog, but she would not walk on it. He recommended surgery, a "tibial plateau leveling osteotomy (TPLO)." The operation was to be done just in time, i.e., before her ligament ruptured.

How could I not do the surgery for this beautiful, three-year old girl? I put half the cost on a credit card and sought the other half through a crowd sourcing venture.

Dixie's recovery included increasingly long leashed walks. By the two-month point, we were at three to four walks a day, each of twenty to thirty minutes. We remained on our three-acre lot. We walked slowly all over it, Dixie leading the way.

It all came to an end one evening. It was our last walk of the day, and I had calculated that another ten minutes or so would tucker her out and we could settle in for the night. I followed her down a particularly steep gully next to a large, old juniper tree. As we neared the bottom, she was ahead of me and passed out of sight around low hanging tree branches. This is the last I remember.

When I came to, I was lying in the dirt. To the best of my reconstruction of the event, Dixie, six feet ahead of me and out of my sight as she rounded the curve of the tree, had spied a rabbit and had taken off in a spectacular leap. In doing so, she had jerked me off my feet. When I came to, I was twenty feet away. I do not recall being dragged. There was no evidence on my coat of being dragged through the red dirt. Is it possible I flew through the air? Or I fast walked until I let go of the leash? I do not know. I was knocked unconscious. When I came to, she was lying next to me.

Stunned, I was able to gather myself a bit. I lifted my head and turned it in her direction. I called her forward, and she belly crawled up to my head. With my left arm, I unhooked her leash. My other arm would not move. Slowly, I got to my knees. Gingerly, wobbling a bit, I got to my feet and stood. My right arm dangled uselessly at my side. The house looked far in the distance. Dixie, also now up, whined at my side. She was unhurt but confused about my behavior. I looked down at her. "Girl," I said, "it's each woman for herself. We have to get to the house." Carefully, slowly we made our way, side by side.

I must have suffered a concussion. What I did after we entered the house was feed Dixie her evening kibble, shrug out of my coat, take two Tylenol and go to bed.

When I woke in the morning, I had a plan. First I had to get Dixie someplace safe and taken care of for an undetermined period of time. Then I had to get to Urgent Care.

I called my nearest neighbors. We had recently worked out arrangements that Linda would care for Dixie while I was on business trips. My call kicked in that arrangement two days early. Left handed, I wrote out a check for ten days of care. Frank and Linda arrived, ready to help in any way they could. "Just Dixie. If you would please take care of her until I get myself straightened out, it would take a lot of worry off my mind." They gathered up Dixie's dog food and bedding. I handed Dixie's leash to Frank. Next to me, she refused to budge. She didn't understand but she knew the mood was ominous.

"Dixie," I said with love and regret in my heart, "You've changed our life together. You have to go with them."

With Dixie taken care of, I turned to my own situation. My arm did not hurt. I knew the matter was serious, however, because it would not move and hung limply at my side. Overnight, dark red-black bruises were showing and swelling had started between my shoulder and the elbow. I called another friend who came to pick me up and accompany me through the day at Urgent Care and then the local hospital's Emergency Room.

The upshot was that the interior of my right shoulder had been shattered. The humeral head was crushed and three quarters of the humerus, the long bone between shoulder and elbow had been damaged. It would require an operation, perhaps the next day, said one doctor. I called my sister and brother in Minnesota. Bernie, now a nurse, flew out the next morning and accompanied me through a week of medical visits and helped me sort out my course of action. Ed and sister-in-law Chris offered to drive and be with me before Bernie left. They were willing to move in with me and help me through what was expected to be an extended recovery period. I cried with gratitude.

The surgery was delayed by almost two weeks. That gave me time to work on Dixie's future.

The first question was whether and how I could get Dixie back into my life. The doctors were shocked I asked the question and adamant in their answer, "The dog that did this? You should never have a dog again, period." One said sharply, "Do you know how many people we see in here with broken bones and other injuries from their dogs? They fell, or were pulled over like you, or tripped over the dog in the night. The danger for you is too great. Don't do it."

I tried anyway. I calculated that my greatest danger was Dixie's strong prey drive. I googled prey drive in dogs and how to retrain the dog. I talked to local dog trainers and veterinarians. The answer I received was that the prey drive cannot be eradicated; it can only be managed. Their training techniques were things I had already been doing: train for a strong recall, and work on "leave it."

I faced the fact that I could not keep her. I had to give Dixie away. I felt horrible, traitorous. I was reminded of Turk, the Golden Retriever that had been taken away from me during my last year of high school. I couldn't believe that I was now a person who was going to surrender their dog. I agonized over what to do.

Who did I know that would possibly adopt Dixie? I had her staying with the most amenable people I knew, yet they were adamant they would not keep her forever. Everyone else I could think of had long ago informed me that Dixie was too large, too exuberant, too much dog for them.

There was a great no-kill animal shelter in Santa Fe. I had already talked to their behavior specialists about Dixie's prey drive; now I asked them about the prognosis for her in the shelter. That's when I learned about Big Black Dog Syndrome in shelters and that black dogs and especially large black dogs were passed over again and again. They stayed long periods of time in the best shelters and at others were quickly put on the euthanasia list. I thought of Dixie's behavior in a small kennel when at the vet. She had banged her tail bloody. "Oh! She's got happy tail," one of the techs said. No, Dixie did not have "happy tail"; she was begging to get out. "I'm a good girl," she was saying, "please let me out. I'm a good girl."

If a shelter would euthanize her after unsuccessful placement attempts, then I should euthanize her now I reasoned and ensure that she did not go through the trauma of being confined in a kennel. With tears streaming down my cheeks, I called my vet and went through my logic with him. He agreed to euthanize Dixie, and I made an appointment for the next day.

I called the neighbors who were caring for Dixie. I asked them to come with me to the vet; I could not manage Dixie on my own. They were out-raged at my choice. "Maybe you could adopt her instead?" I asked, hoping against hope. Again, sobbing, I went through my logic. I was facing surgery and long term recovery. The prognosis for a full recovery was not good. I could not care for Dixie. I was adamant that I was not going to surrender her to a shelter. I had no one who would take her long term. What was the responsible thing to do? We ended the conversation with their reluctant agreement to accompany me to the vet's office.

They called back within half an hour. "OK, if you sign her over to us, we promise we will find a good home for her. Meantime, she will stay here. If it is impossible to find a home for her, we will keep her."

The relief I felt! Now I was really crying. "Thank you. Thank you."

With a glad heart, I began my treatment plan. Surgery, quiet recovery, hours of physical therapy. After a month or so, I could dress myself one handed. Sometimes, I found myself staring out the living room window imagining I could see through the tall wooden fence and see what Dixie was doing.

I arranged with Frank and Linda to have a day with Dixie. Linda walked her over. I thought Dixie would be excited to be back in her big yard. But she calmly sniffed through the house and then lay down in the living room. When Linda left, I walked with Dixie to our favorite place. I sat on the wrought iron loveseat facing the Sangre de Cristos, and she jumped up be-side me. She sat upright and I put my good arm around her and hugged her to me. She turned and gave me a lick on the face. She'd never done that before.

We sat there quietly and then walked on just the flat land around the house. I was no longer venturing up and down the rocky lot. Dixie, like me, was subdued. She went over to sniff around the shed and then came back. We went inside. I rested on the couch. She sprawled on the floor next to me.

When Linda came back, Dixie got up and left with no hesitation. During the day I had felt the history of our bond together. Now, I also felt that for her, at least, the detachment process had begun.

After six weeks, Frank and Linda told me they had found a home for Dixie. They described it: a three-person family, husband, wife and teenage son. All adults, no one Dixie would knock over. The man was retired so Dixie would have someone around most of the time. The family was experienced as dog owners. They asked me for the last time: Do you want Dixie back?

I knew with even greater certainty that I could not be responsible for a ninety-pound dog. "No. Thank you for finding a home for her. When she's settled and I'm feeling better, can I come see her in her new home?"

"Sure," Frank said, "we'll all go together. She'll like that."

Meanwhile, my recovery was *not* going smoothly. I was in constant pain. My visits from caretakers and well-wishers had long ago ceased. Much of my life was now totally structured around my daily needs. Showering and washing my hair was an especially onerous task. Preparing meals, eating and cleaning up took many more hours in my achingly slow mode. I continued formal physical therapy for seven months and then continued with hours of PT exercises at home until finally everyone said that was as far as I was going to get. I could manage quite adequately, but the top shelf cupboards would be forever out of reach.

I waited three months for Dixie to get settled in before I asked if I could see her. "They say no, Jude. It's taken awhile to deal with her separation anxiety. Maybe later." There was no later. Despite my numerous but carefully spaced requests, Dixie's new owners did not want to chance her having contact with me. They thought it would jeopardize their relationship with her. I knew it wouldn't. I believed Dixie was happy and loved. Seeing her would have been for me, for closure. I wanted the reconciliation to deal with my guilt in surrendering her. I wasn't going to get it that way. I settled into the realization that she was fine. I had to heal myself.

I was lonely. No Dixie. No Tigger. Every task was an effort that had to be planned and then rested from. Outdoors, it was quiet, too. A large jackrabbit began to come around. Bernie named him Jack Black when I told her about his frequent visits. Daily, I poured water into the large flat metal well cover in the yard. Mountain bluebirds and robins came in huge numbers—fifty or more at a time to drink and splash. I sat on the deck and read about healing physically and mentally from trauma. I realized I had had many traumas to grieve and to heal, not only these most recent ones of shattering my shoulder and surrendering Dixie.

The loss of Dixie marked a huge transition. I had lost so many things in my life, from trust in my mother's love to belief in my husband. From those betrayals I had turned to my dogs and their unconditional love. That was not a guarantee to not feel pain, however. The loss of each dog whether from death or forced separation hurt me profoundly. After I had originally re-solved to not be hurt again, I had shunned dogs in my life for the next thirty years. Then I opened my heart to that black collie pup and a charismatic and callous man.

In the past, I had not taken time to reflect on and assess these experi-ences. When young, school and work had allowed me to remain numb. For the next three decades, I had maintained a career woman, road warrior life-style. My work hours—seventy to ninety a week—consumed my time. Later, when I had slowed my work life to make time for a family, there had been no abatement in the number of hours spent on others. The dual role had exhausted me. Then divorce, additional lawsuits and disabilities had con-sumed my time. Dixie had stopped me in my tracks and pulled me up short. I could not go back to my old life.

This time with no dog led me to reflect deeply into myself. Grief, I recog-nized, is a part of life. You cannot avoid it. Best to meet it head on. As I heard once, "Invite your grief to tea." I did that many a day during my recovery.

I thought about Dixie and acknowledged the guilt I felt in having sur-rendered her. I sat with that feeling. Only then was I able to come to an un-derstanding that Dixie's needs and my travel lifestyle were not a good fit. As in my marriage, I had tried and tried to force a match where there was none. Sometimes, no matter how hard you work at it, it's just not right.

Finally, I heard from Dixie's new owners. Through Frank and Linda, they said, "Tell Jude that Dixie is doing fine. She's calmed down a lot. Someone is almost always home with her. We love her. We all love her."

I believe that Dixie had indeed found the right home for her. Now, I needed to find the right life for me.

Lacey, Service Dog

April 28, 2013 to the present

To combat the loneliness I was feeling during and after recovery from my shattered shoulder, and to be near dogs since I had been advised by my doctors to never have another dog, I began to volunteer at the Santa Fe Animal Shelter. I did administrative work.

The Shelter was well run and well resourced. This plus their willingness to travel led them to drive to other areas of the country to rescue dogs and cats likely to be euthanized in their home habitat. They mixed these often small dogs in with their more standard Pit Bulls, Rottweilers and Cattle Dogs. Sometimes the small fluffy dogs attracted members of the public who then adopted a larger dog once face-to-face with the sad eyes and hopeful look of a longtime shelter resident.

Lacey was such a dog, who by being transported from one shelter to another managed to continue to live and have a chance at a forever home.

◇◇◇◇◇◇◇◇◇◇◇◇◇◇◇◇◇◇◇◇◇◇

In my year and a half without a dog, I missed having a dog like crazy. At that time, I was sixty-five years old. I had successfully navigated a painful, recriminatory divorce. The divorce, and the marriage, had scorched my finances. I was making my way up out of a deep, black marital well. Some days I felt like I was at the bottom of the well still, searching for a rope with which to pull myself out. Other days, more days now, I felt like I was sitting on the edge of the well wall, dangling my feet. I had been successful in extracting myself from the perils of deep, dark water, but I was not yet strong enough to scamper off and away.

Periodically I would walk one of the calmest dogs at the shelter to test my ability to handle a dog. The dogs I tested got smaller and smaller, and still my shoulder would ache after only a few minutes into the walk. One afternoon after walking one lovely but persistent and strong shelter dog, I bemoaned my ability to find a dog that would work with my latest medical condition. "I'm a large dog person! Now I'm walking dogs of only thirty-five pounds and they are still too much for me. I'll never have a dog again!" Despite doctors' orders, though, I was still hopeful about changing my dog-less state.

I discussed various small dog breeds with Dylan, the adoption manager. I poo-pooed one breed after another. "Well, a Miniature Poodle might be OK. But what shelter has a poodle? And it's a foo-foo dog, anyway," I whined. "I want a working dog breed." I remembered that my first dog was a Cocker Spaniel. Paddy had been an amazing dog, comparable in my mind to Lassie, the dog of my childhood television programs. "Well, I did have a Cocker Spaniel once. He was a great dog. And spaniels *look* like dogs."

I didn't realize I had left Dylan with the picture of a spaniel for me in his mind. Nor did I realize that in one of the back isolation kennels was a little black and white spaniel from Los Angeles recovering from a respiratory disease. "Lacey" had kept her name from LA to Santa Fe. A few days after my conversation with Dylan, the shelter vets released her from quarantine, and she was transferred out of medical and into the adoption department.

When the text from Dylan came in, it said, "Your dog is here." I saw the anxious eyes of a black-and-white-faced spaniel of some determination. I closed the picture and pulled my attention back to the business meeting in front of me. In the back of my mind, however, thoughts were racing. "Is this my dog? Now that the opportunity presents itself, do I *really* want a dog? Can I handle a dog with this shoulder and the limitations I have? Can I *afford* a dog?"

Managing the responsibility of a dog is life changing from that of no dog. There I was in Albuquerque, having been gone from home for what would have been six to seven hours. Was this dog a puppy that required close attention? And the cost of a dog! Dixie had eaten enormous amounts of food and was accident prone. I had had huge vet bills. My finances were still precarious.

I woke up the next morning still uncertain. My day was jam-packed with work appointments and deadlines. "I don't have time to think about this!" I worked through the day, the little dog shunted to the back of my mind. The following morning was a Saturday. I woke early and lay in bed. "What should I do? What should I do?"

"Well," I resolved, "I have to at least see the dog." I threw off the covers and quickly dressed. I realized it would be wise to call the shelter and tell the adoption counselors on duty of my interest in the black and white spaniel that had recently been moved into adoptions.

"Jude, we've got that huge adoption event in Albuquerque this morning. That dog has already been brought down there. She's probably set up by now and is available for adoption!"

"Oh, no!" I said. "I don't know for sure that I want her but I need to see her."

"I'll call down there. Maybe she can be put on 'hold' for an hour or two. How long will it take you to get down there?"

"I'm grabbing my car keys now. Not too much longer than an hour." I must have had some suspicion of what was going to happen because before I left I went out to the shed and rummaged through old boxes of dog supplies and gathered two collars of different sizes and a leather leash. I discarded the idea of a crate but grabbed some cross ties and two or three towels to put in the seat of the car. I dashed out the door and was on my way.

The drive to Albuquerque was seventy-five-mile-per-hour interstate driving, yet it felt like it was taking a very long time, too long. Would the dog still be there? Had the shelter managed to reach the offsite staff and did they agree to wait for me? I drove faster.

My thoughts warred between anxiety about whether with my physical handicaps I could manage the responsibilities of having a dog and excitement that perhaps my time of living alone was over. "Jude, you can't afford a dog. You're just getting back on your feet financially…. Do you really want to sweep the kitchen floor twice a day like you did when Dixie was there? A dog will curtail your ability to do things. How long can you leave a small dog alone?" Then the other side of the argument, "I need a watch dog. With only one functioning ear, I can't hear an approaching car. It is scary at night." (I chose the most "reasonable" rationale for a dog as my first argument.) "A dog is companionship, someone else to pay attention to—not only myself. A dog is unconditional love!" I laughed at myself. "Let's see this dog first. If she makes me smile, then I'll think about taking her."

The adoption event was held on the extensive grassy grounds of the Albuquerque hot air balloon museum park. The parking lot was huge and jam-packed with cars, trucks and the vans and trailers from twelve to fifteen animal adoption agencies around the region. How was I going to find the Santa Fe shelter location?

I called the shelter office again. "I'm here. I'm in the parking lot. Did they hold the dog for me? Where are the Santa Fe shelter dogs? It's crazy out here!"

"Yes. They're in a big white tent; the tent is way in the back. The volunteer coordinator said she would recognize you. Walk into the park area. There is a main aisle. Start down the aisle. Elizabeth will find you."

I did as I was told. There were so many big white tents! Most of the tents were open sided, and inviting to walk into and see the dogs. (I didn't see any cats.) Within each tent, I saw dogs grouped together in temporary fencing. Sometimes there was a person with a "volunteer" tag, either holding a dog or showing it to a prospective adopter. I realized that many, many shelters and rescue groups were using this opportunity to showcase their dogs and find suitable homes for them. In response, the public was there in droves. There was a carnival feeling in the air. Dogs were being walked; some potential adopters had brought their current dogs to do a "meet and greet" with a possible adoption candidate. Small children were in strollers, some with tiny caps on their heads to block the sun, which was already strong; other children were toddling along at the hand of a parent, eyes wide at all the activity.

"Jude! This way. Quick!" Elizabeth had come out of nowhere and now she had me by my elbow. The crowd was so numerous I was glad she recognized me. I hadn't seen her. "Your little dog is very popular. There are three people lined up already to adopt her. They are getting irritated. Hurry!"

We hastened up the aisle between the tents. Elizabeth guided me under a canvas flap into the cool dark of one of the larger tents. I saw five or six circular three-foot high temporary fencing "dog yards." I didn't see the dog I was looking for. Elizabeth guided me through the maze to the far corner. There, in a six-foot diameter round pen were three small dogs. One was black and white and had long, curly hair. She looked about a year old. That must be the dog. I watched her. Did she feel my eyes on her? She did, because she crossed the pen and sat down in front of me, looking at me expectantly. I heard her question in my mind: "Are you the one I'm waiting for?"

A staff person asked me, "Do you want to walk her?" I broke out of my daze. "Yes. Yes! Of course." Her leash was put in my hand. "There is a grassy area over there—through the tent and behind that large truck. Take her out there. She'll benefit from a break."

What did she do that day that captured my heart immediately? I'm not sure, but as we walked out of the tent, I was already feeling joyous. I called back to the staff counselor, "You can tell those people to find another dog. This one's mine!" Being able to claim Lacey was a great benefit of my many volunteer hours with the shelter.

We walked a bit. Lacey enjoyed sniffing the grass and, I imagine, feeling the warm sunshine on her back after weeks indoors in a kennel. I called to her. She turned and raced back to me. She jumped on me, reaching my knees, her long, "lacey" tail wagging back and forth full throttle. I got down on one knee and hugged her. I felt quickly bonded with her.

I filled out the paperwork and made my payment. I slipped the smaller of the two collars I had brought around Lacey's neck and attached my leash. We were on our way!

As we walked out of the grassy park area, we passed an attendant station at the entrance to the park. The attendant called out, "Is that Lacey?" What? My dog is known to everyone? I was astounded. "I walked her this morning as we were getting set up. She's a sweetheart." I waved to the attendant as Lacey led me with determination out of that crowded, noisy area and into the greater quiet of the parking lot. "OK, girl. I get it. We're out of here. My car is over there. Have you ever been in a car? We're going to find out."

Since we had just had a walk, I thought Lacey was ready to get into the car. But where to put her? My big dogs had gone in through the hatchback of the Subaru. But I had just found her! I couldn't leave this little girl in the back of the car all by herself. I encouraged Lacey into the front passenger seat of the car. With my shoulder damage I knew I couldn't lift her. She seemed to know what I wanted and she scrambled in and up onto the seat.

She was so small. She didn't take up but half the bottom seat cushion! Now, how to affix her in her seat? I wrapped her in a combo of car seat belt and cross ties with clips on each end. OK. We were ready to go.

For that first month or so with Lacey I was working at home, so Lacey and I had time to get acquainted. I've never had a dog that was so easy to train. First, her name. I decided to keep the name she had at the shelter, it fit her, her physical appearance and her lighthearted personality.

I was surprised she didn't know her name. Everybody else knew her name! Then I remembered she hadn't had much interaction with dogs or people since being at the Santa Fe shelter. She had been in quarantine with a respiratory infection almost all of that time. To teach her name, I used the technique that had worked with my dogs before her. I sat cross-legged on the floor, facing her, with a handful of tasty low-calorie treats next to me. I held out one tidbit, allowed her to take it and at the same time said her name clearly and firmly. "Lacey." Again. I gave her a treat and said "Lacey." Over and over again. She was a food-focused dog, so training with treats worked well with her. She learned her name that night in one session.

Lacey got me outside. I had been indoors over the winter, spending my early morning quiet time at the east-facing window. It felt like I had been at that window for the year and a half since my shoulder accident. I wasn't aware of it at the time, but like many people after an accident, I had become fearful. I was fearful of walking on uneven ground. I was fearful of going up and down steps. I was afraid I would trip and hurt myself again. I was extremely cautious, and as I realized later, I had greatly limited my world because of my fears.

Lacey had been spayed two days before the adoption event. Our first two weeks were spent with her on leashed walks only, eight to ten times a day. It reminded me of that last walk with Dixie where I fell. My lot is crumbly dirt, shale, easy to slip on. I was afraid to walk her. Every step was a reminder of my crash with Dixie and resulting shattered shoulder. With Lacey, I was very careful. If there was a message from her, it was, "Wear the right shoes!" Walking day after day with Lacey, I learned better techniques for walking over rough terrain and I regained my confidence.

Because of my experience with my other dogs and classroom training with them, I was confident in teaching Lacey basic obedience commands. She seemed to have the idea of "sit." Certainly not a crisp sit like my prior dog trainers required, though, so we improved on that, again using small treats for her little twenty-pound body.

"Wait" was a fun command to teach. I did it with Lacey fastened in the front seat in her car seat harness. When I took her into town with me on errand runs and I got out of the car, I said, "Wait," knowing she was locked in. When I got out of the car to open the gate, "Wait," I would say and pet her excitedly when I returned. "Good wait!" Then it became easy to do it in the house. "Wait" at the front door while I opened it. "OK" to tell her she could cross the threshold. One time, she scampered through the door, not "waiting" and quickly went to check on her favorite toy. Then she dashed back outside where I was still standing at the front door and she sat, tail thumping, waiting for the OK command.

It did take a lot of time adjusting to a new, untrained dog. Those early days of a dog entering one's house are important. I had to find the time to work with her and not let bad habits develop. I had several work projects to do at home. It was good to not have to travel and leave her somewhere under another person's care. But my project work and thus my billable hours suffered those first few months after Lacey arrived at my house.

Lacey was about a year old when we met. I was unaware of her prior experiences, but I could tell that while she was extremely good natured, she was not trained. Training did come easily, though. She's smart, food oriented and eager to please. She does, however, also have a stubborn streak that she shows when there is something she wants and it is not what I want.

As our routine settled into place, and she and I became comfortable and trusting of each other, I looked around for a group dog training class. One of the dog trainers I met through my work at the shelter was starting a Canine Good Citizen training course, and I decided to enroll.

The Canine Good Citizen training, test and certificate program is probably the most common and familiar dog training program in the U.S. Designed and managed by the American Kennel Club, the test consists of ten challenges that the dog must be able to accomplish when tested by a qualified evaluator. The purpose of the training is to cultivate a pet dog that is relaxed in common situations and obedient to basic commands. In other words, a dog that is a pleasure to be around.

Lacey did well in her training and passed the Canine Good Citizen test. I was lucky that day because she does have one flaw: she does not meet new dogs trustingly, especially if they are larger than her. She will sometimes growl, and this is grounds for failing the test. To continue to participate in group training and in particular to address this issue of Lacey's, we took the class a second time. This time, Lacey served as a good role model for the new dogs in the class.

One morning after class, Helen, the dog trainer, remarked on my hearing loss (it had become total deafness in one ear and some loss in the other). She called it a disability. I was shocked. I did not think of myself as "disabled." She suggested we train Lacey as my service dog. "She's smart enough," Helen said. "I can help you. And you know, Jude, your hearing loss is only going to get worse as you get older. Do it now while Lacey is young and easily trained, and you are high functioning."

First I had to get used to the idea of being disabled in order to think of having a service dog. Her statement challenged me in a way I hadn't addressed previously—that was to publicly acknowledge my hearing loss. I thought I had dealt as well as possible with my loss of hearing functionality. I had researched and procured treatment for it. I had adjusted my work life and day-to-day lifestyle to accommodate it. I recalled that it hadn't been easy to acknowledge to myself that I had a hearing loss. Five years ago, when I woke up with no hearing in my right ear and with my head congested, I thought I had a head cold sufficiently serious that it was affecting my hearing. I waited several weeks for the "cold" to clear up. When I went to the ENT doctor, I learned about Sudden Hearing Loss. I took it as a problem to be addressed, but not a problem to let the world know about.

The doctor said I was fortunate to be able to benefit from hearing aids since not all hearing impaired people can. I did not feel "benefited"; I did not see myself as a person who wore hearing aids!

And, how visible would they be? Did everyone need to know that I was an *old* person with a hearing problem? Turns out I was not a candidate for in-the-ear hearing aids. Mine, one especially, were large and went behind my ear with a wire and post threaded into the ear canal. The first thing I did was make sure I had a hair cut that hid the hearing aids so that few people noticed them. People only knew I had a disability if I told them. Instead of telling folks, I would say casually, "Here, sit over here." Sometimes I did say, "Could you speak louder, I can't hear you."

Also the cost! Hearing aids, like canes and walkers, are not covered by insurance. The first hearing aid I got was a single one and amplified sound for the ear that had significant loss. However, within a year, whatever remnants of hearing capability that had been in that ear were gone. I learned that improvements had been made for a "crossover" hearing aid and were just being released. I still would have a hearing aid in my right ear, but its purpose would be to transmit sound from that area to my left, hearing ear. When all was well and done, I had spent 7,000 precious dollars on hearing aids. I was fortunate that insurance did cover the multitude of tests I had taken to try to determine the cause and type of hearing loss I had. The outcome of these tests still was the inexplicable: Sudden Hearing Loss diagnosis.

So, I had acknowledged to myself that I had a hearing loss. I had worked the problem and come up with a solution—hearing aids that increased my functionality but did not return my hearing to normal. I wasn't aware I had more to acknowledge.

Now, several years had gone by, and Helen was calling it a disability. This was something else altogether. She was telling me that I fit the category of people who are disabled. OK, "high functioning disabled." That way of thinking about myself was a shock.

Eventually an incident occurred that finally convinced me I had to do more about my hearing loss. A hail storm had damaged my shingle roof sufficiently for the insurance company to agree to replace it in its entirety. That was scheduled to occur one day a few months after Lacey came to live with me. I had work to do so I closed all the window blinds so as to not be distracted by the comings and goings of the workmen.

Lacey was loose in the house but under my supervision. At one point in the early afternoon, she barked insistently. I looked up from my desk. "It's OK, little girl. We're getting a new roof." She quieted and I worked for several more hours.

Later in the day, neighbor Linda called. "I bet you are glad to have that truck gone. It was so loud! The beep-beep-beep drove *me* crazy."

"What truck?" I asked.

It turns out that the shingles had been delivered by a large flatbed truck with a hoist at the back end. When the truck went into reverse, as it did several times to get positioned next to the house as well as when the hoist lifted packets of shingles, a loud beep-beep-beep was sounded. We worked out that the timing of the truck's activity was when Lacey was barking in the house to alert me. I was dumbfounded that my hearing was so hampered that I had not heard the truck. That was when I decided to accept Helen's offer of training Lacey as my service dog.

I am a disabled person who does not have an outward manifestation of disability. I had been able to hide, to "pass" if you will. I could appear normal, able bodied. For me, a service dog vest on Lacey would trumpet to the world that I was a disabled person. And on top of that, with not being visibly disabled, people would be skeptical of my need for a service dog. They would see me in the category of "faker."

And Lacey doesn't look like a service dog. She's not the German Shepherd or Labrador Retriever that you normally see. She's a twenty-pound spaniel mix with a sweet face that people call "adorable." Not only did I have to publicly own up to the label *disabled*, I had to do it with a service dog that looked like Aunt Tillie's lap dog! Well, this called for yet another mental and emotional shift!

Although I had long been aware of service dogs and had read stories about their oftentimes heroic behavior, I didn't really know much beyond the fact that service dogs aid the blind. I read up a bit, and learned that the type of service animal I would be using was a "hearing alert service dog."

Once I had accepted the idea, I cleared my schedule for structured training. Helen and I met every Sunday morning for a year. During the week, Lacey and I practiced daily what we had learned. I resolved that Lacey's first service would be to alert me to the teapot whistle. I love to drink coffee in the morning, and for thirty years I have made pour-over, drip style coffee. Unfortunately, sometimes, I do not hear the tea pot whistle go off and I lose water, or worse, boil all of the water out of the pot. Numerous people have told me to just get an electric coffee pot, but they miss the point, and I thought this would be a good start for Lacey and me.

Actually it took us six weeks to get this task down pat. I started with Lacey and me comfortable on a couch in the living room, within easy sight and sound of the kitchen and the teapot. When the tea kettle whistled, I jumped off the couch and ran to the stove, yelling excitedly to Lacey who ran with me. At the stove, I gave Lacey a high value treat, praised her greatly and turned the tea kettle off. We did this for days, weeks actually, before Lacey seemed to get what I wanted. I thought we had this exercise nailed, when one day, I was in my bedroom making the bed and Lacey was in the living room. The tea kettle went off and Lacey raced from the couch to the stove, just as I had taught her. However, she had forgotten me! Needless to say, we modified the training technique with her coming to me first, the true "alert," at which time I gave her a treat and then we went to the kitchen stove with the "show me" command and another treat there. Soon she did have the exercise mastered, and I was greatly pleased for us both. It was a humbling experience to recognize the logical, literal thinking of the dog and realize that although she was willing, I had to learn to train in a way that made sense to her. Thereafter, I trained in chunks of small tasks.

Helen frequently said that the first task is the hardest to train, and she was right. Once we had the tea kettle whistle alert in place, it was easy to teach Lacey to alert me when the phone, alarm clock, oven timer, smoke detector, or door bell went off. Paired with the "show me" command, I could find the cell phone—what a wonderful convenience when one cannot tell what direction a sound is coming from or determine which kitchen alarm is going off!

There are three components to training a service dog: basic obedience training; public access training; and then the specific disability task training.

In a popular TV show, Brandon McMillan uses his "seven common commands" as his obedience training structure: sit, stay, down, come, off, heel, no. I use those commands, and I've added: wait, leave it, take it, walk on, watch me and that wonderful all-purpose OK. Lacey also allows me to wipe her feet one by one when we come in from outside. She waits at the base of the couch for "OK" before she jumps up and joins me.

As we worked on the obedience commands, we interlaced the "public access" commands every service dog must master. Lacey had to operate calmly and confidently in strange, noisy and crowded places. Helen and I took her to big box home repair supply stores, looking for the loudest, most startling noises the store could provide. We went to the airport and watched the baggage roll down the chute. We rode elevators up and down. We walked along heavily trafficked streets. We sat on city bus benches and watched police cars and fire trucks scream past. By going slowly and starting from a distance, Lacey came to feel comfortable in these alarming situations.

About three months into Lacey's public access training, I put her "Service Dog in Training" vest on her and we went on a two-night trip to Taos, a nearby touristy arts town. We arrived in the parking lot of the hotel I had booked. I unhooked her car harness and put on her walking collar and service vest. Off we went into the hotel lobby to check in.

I hadn't realized how many of her trained commands she had to pull off perfectly just for us to check in! To perform public access tasks properly, Lacey had to operate in a brand new environment with strangers present, and in this case, construction going on in the parking lot and near the registration desk.

Lacey had to calmly perform:

1) Controlled unload out of a vehicle; waiting for and following instruction before leaving her seat

2) Approach to a building; crossing the parking lot without fear regardless of moving vehicles

3) Controlled entry through a doorway; no pushing, shoving, or dawdling

4) Heeling through a building; stay with me, girl!

5) Sitting on command; staying in place even when I drop the leash to have better access to my purse for driver's license and credit card

6) Not being distracted by nearby noises; here it was construction sounds and strangers in clomping boots and hard hats

7) Controlled exit; calmly exiting the hotel and crossing the parking lot

8) Controlled load into a vehicle; being willing and timely

9) Team relationship, e.g., me being able to address requests for verification or documentation of my service dog's status per the ADA (American Disability Act) requirements; her demonstrating being a bonded partner to me

All this occurred while she and I were being scrutinized by passersby, as every handler/service dog team is when in public. "Is that a service dog?" a question frequently asked with some excitement. Or, "Is that *really* a service dog?" asked with skepticism.

We checked in successfully, Lacey only deviating from perfection by looking around with great interest while I talked with the front desk clerk. And then she performed those tasks again, when we re-parked the car near our assigned room and I brought our luggage in.

She performed additional public access tasks, including good restaurant behavior, while we were on our mini-vacation. The only time we received truly nasty looks was from suspicious clerks when we went into a bookstore. From that "vacation," I came to realize that being a service dog is hard work. Lacey and I incorporated a nap into each day to be refreshed for the evening activities.

All in all, we spent more than 600 hours in training activities before I re-read the service dog and hearing alert dog requirements and realized that we had done it all! Helen did a final test. Part of the public access test was walking calmly through a crowded Trader Joe's store. Lacey aced it!

I know a woman who told me "I have a service dog! I bought a service dog vest online. I just have to put it on my dog and I can go anywhere!" She laughed. When I first heard that several years ago, I was annoyed and somewhat embarrassed for her. Now, after the hours and hours of training that Lacey and I have had to ensure our mutual aid and safety and to perform unobtrusively in public, I get angry when I hear those remarks, particularly if the dog referred to is ill mannered and smearing the reputation of "real" service dogs.

Because I wanted to think some more about the difficulty I had experienced acknowledging publicly that I am handicapped, I asked my friend Diane to talk about her experiences. We met over a cup of coffee and a slice of carrot cake. Diane became blind two years ago, caused by eye strokes after a fall. In very strong light, she can see movement of shapes, but no facial features or details of any sort. I could easily eat more of the carrot cake than she could find on the plate. I try to be fair.

Looking at her, you can't tell she is blind. She wears transitional glasses that turn into sunglasses outside and look like regular glasses when she is inside. For other health reasons, she does walk with a cane, but it is a beautiful, colorful cane, not the black with white tip cane that signals a blind person. I asked her to help me think about why it is difficult to be public about one's disability.

"People treat you differently," she said immediately. "Some people think if you can't see or if you can't hear that you've lost your mental faculties. That happened to me a few days ago when I got a manicure. The attendant treated me like an idiot.

"I am, of course, slower with some things, like my iPhone. It is difficult when you can't see the icons. But I can learn. And I remember well. I hate it when some impatient person pulls the phone out of my hand, punches buttons and then returns it to me with exasperation, 'Here, now it is ready.' How can I learn when they do that?

"And friends disappear. I know it is more difficult to be with me. I do need some help. In this restaurant, for example, you helped me with a ride here, making my way to the table and reading the menu. You don't need to feed me (I surreptitiously took another bite of carrot cake), and I can carry on a perfectly good conversation. I still have something to contribute!"

Diane had had a career involving many of the socially active and influential people in Albuquerque. "Walking out of this restaurant, finding our way between the tightly packed tables," she said, "I fear hearing someone say, 'Isn't that Diane? Whatever has happened to her? She used to be so active and vibrant. Now she has to be helped out!'"

When Diane walks with her hand nestled in the arm of her husband, they have more finesse and panache than I show walking with her. I feel apprehensive, aware of chairs that have been left pushed into the aisle, people standing who step back without looking behind them first. I know I add to the awkwardness and "public-ness" of her disability.

"There are advantages of people knowing you are blind," I say. "For example, you ask the wait person to identify the location of each food item on your plate when they put your plate in front of you. Nine times out of ten they don't understand why you are asking until you say that you are blind. If they knew when they set the plate down, they might know to provide you with that information."

"I think people, especially young, healthy people," she said, "could be more aware that many people have an infirmity of one sort or another and not assume that everyone is as strong or healthy as they are." We laugh remembering times we've dined together, her blind, me with my shoulder in a sling and a wait person put the ketchup or salt at the far end of the table, out of her sight or my reach.

"Having a dog makes a huge difference in my life." Diane is referring to the comfort and companionship she receives from her pet dog, a six-year-old terrier mix. While quite sensitive to Diane's moods, Abby's temperament does not make her a candidate for a service dog. Nevertheless, I well understand the bond that can develop between a human and a canine. Diane and Abby have a special relationship.

I finish my coffee, and push the carrot cake back toward Diane. As we rise, Lacey quietly gets up from her place tucked under the table. Few people in the restaurant knew she was there. The three of us make our exit, Lacey in the lead, checking for obstacles and once outside, for any unheard, unseen cars coming through the parking lot.

I think how fortunate I am. Lacey is young, now only three. I hope to have many more quality years with her. Meanwhile she has already helped me with important life lessons. Her obvious role is to help me with my physical interface with the world. I thought it was only my right arm and shoulder physical handicap I had to conquer to manage having a dog. Lacey helped me acknowledge and then overcome the insidious residue of fear that often remains after a fall. Now I walk several times a day with Lacey and I love it!

To responsibly take advantage of the opportunity of having a service dog, I had to publicly acknowledge my hearing disability and integrate that disability graciously into my sense of who I am and how others see me. Lacey helped me with that, too. Well done, Lacey.

Lacey. In service. Of service.

Good dog, Lacey.

Epilogue

December 2016 – February 2018

I had known for quite a while that I would eventually settle down in Minnesota. The breakup of my marriage led me to it along with my concerns about the availability and quality of health care. The fact that my siblings and longtime friends from Minnesota were willing to visit me in New Mexico but were not willing to move had something to do with it, too. Perhaps the fact that I had to hire my handyman to get a drive to and from my brain MRI settled it.

But I was in no hurry. How I loved my northern New Mexico corner of the world! My house had glorious views of gold and purple sunrises and fiery sunsets—almost every day! My lot was totally fenced in and trenched after Dancer proved to be such an escape artist. It was like having my own three-acre dog park that Lacey and I could stroll through several times a day. (I strolled. Lacey scampered.)

So when I went to Minnesota for family visits, I took advantage of the time to look at possible new life options. I remember looking at detached houses when Dixie was my dog. During my no-dog time before Lacey, I began to look at senior housing. I had reached the age of sixty-five, and if I was living in Minnesota it seemed best to not be responsible for snow shoveling. None of the buildings I looked at had any particular appeal for me, or didn't fit my pocketbook, until I discovered the cooperative housing market designed for seniors in the Twin Cities of Minneapolis–Saint Paul. In the 1970s, I had lived in a Washington, D.C. housing cooperative. The philosophy of "together and separate" resonated with me.

I continued my review of options after Lacey became my dog. With a service dog, I had the option of moving into not pet friendly locations. I quickly backed away from this possibility after I felt the venom of residents who had made their no-pets choice and resented being encroached upon.

By December 2016, I had settled on pet friendly independent living for seniors in housing cooperatives as the option I was most interested in. I found some that fulfilled many of my requirements. I put down a waiting list deposit on several, even the "pet friendly" co-op that required the resident dogs to cross the common area in a stroller so that the carpet never had dog feet on it. I assumed that my service dog status would exempt me from that foo-foo policy. Since the building was near several longtime friends and had an adjacent park area, I put myself on their waiting list.

In preparation for my 2016 Christmas visit to Minnesota, I identified a few more of the remaining senior co-ops that I had not yet examined and set up a visit schedule. One day I had two appointments. My longtime friend, Michele, offered to accompany me in my search that day.

My morning appointment was one that I had scheduled several weeks before. "I have a service dog," I dutifully reported, "and I am looking for a pet friendly building." "Oh yes! We'll be glad to give you a tour. We have several openings."

The time for the appointment came. Michele, Lacey and I exited our car and crossed the icy parking lot to the front door of the co-op. I rang the bell. I saw a young woman leave her office and come to the front door.

She opened the door a crack.

"Hello," I said cheerily. "I'm Jude. I have an appointment for a tour."

The woman stared down at Lacey. "He can't come in here. Dogs have to enter through the back door."

Patiently, I informed her, "Lacey is a service dog. We have an appointment." I waited with my smile pasted on my face.

"He can't come in here!" she said shrilly, sticking to policy as best she knew it. I stared at her in disbelief. I turned to Michele who likewise was dumbfounded. In my mind, I fast forwarded to what it would be like if Lacey and I lived in this building. "You know, this is not a place we want to live." The three of us turned around and re-crossed the parking lot to our car. We went for an early lunch.

I admit my spirits were a bit dampened after that experience. Michele encouraged me to keep the second appointment. It was a senior housing co-op I had just heard about from my sister. I had made an appointment only the afternoon before. "You won't be back for a while," Michele pointed out. "Let's do it now and check it out."

Again we pulled into an icy parking lot and headed to the front door. Lacey led the way. This time the door was opened for us. "Is this Lacey?" exclaimed Debbie, the Resident Services Manager. "And are you Jude? Welcome! Come in. Come in."

"Hi. I'm Brad and I'm on the Board of Directors." He shook my hand, then Michele's. "Hi! I'm Joan. I'm just collecting my mail but I'll tell you—you won't find a nicer place than this anywhere." There were six or seven additional people in the little lobby located between several open common spaces. Some were there to collect their mail; others had congregated to greet their neighbors. One man squatted down in front of Lacey and spoke to her kindly, "Hello, little girl." He looked up at me, "If you ever need a pet sitter or a dog walker, I'm your man. I live on the first floor."

I was flabbergasted at the goodwill shown to us and the camaraderie among the co-op members present. I looked at Michele. She opened her eyes wide to say, "Well, this is certainly different than the last place!"

As it turned out, there was a unit available. It was more spacious than I had thought I could afford and less costly than I had budgeted. It had a deck for Lacey and a garage space for the Subaru. I put my name on the waiting list.

It was the Winter Solstice of 2016.

The ten people on the waiting list before me fell like dominoes. My house in Santa Fe sold in four days and for more money than I had dreamed possible. Lacey and I were living in our new home in April.

Today, Lacey sits next to me on the couch. It is the middle of the night. I was awakened by ghost dog memories; they swirl around me. How fortunate I have been to have so many wonderful dogs in my life!

I've heard many people say over the years, "I'll never have another dog. It hurt too much when Sugar/Rex/Lucy died." I made the same choice and for thirty years I did not have a dog. Then it was wonderful when Bear entered my life! Next Muggles and Paddy. The Three Musketeers. Just thinking about them and their antics as pals puts a huge smile on my face. The three of them appeared in a dream to me not too long ago. They were together. They wanted me to know they were together and that they will be welcoming me when my time comes to cross the Rainbow Bridge.

Dancer.… I suspect he is caught between Paddy and waiting for Dixie. Such a big, strong dog Dixie was but she did much better when she was under Dancer's guidance. He knows that.

This legacy of seven great dogs has led me to Lacey—and what a special little dog she is! How privileged I am to be with her.

My lifestyle has changed now. Working and writing from home, I have daily time to be with my dog. Since she is a service dog, she accompanies me most times when I leave the apartment. When she sits for her meal, I see the long legacy of dogs before her, going back to Paddy, the Wonder Dog, and Turk, My Golden Boy.

I've come to understand the special pleasures of a small dog. For one, there is a greater physical closeness. Like a large cat, Lacey lies across my lap as I write here or she cuddles next to me as I watch evening TV. Lacey is amazed that so many dogs and so many people can live together in one building. She thinks it is grand and has expanded her scope of responsibility to include everyone.

What an experience this has been to conjure up my canine pals out of the mists of the past! I pulled out old journals and calendars and gleaned stories about each of them. I sat in reverie and just remembered. I cried and I laughed. I made notes and pieced together recollections. These were my best friends at significant times in my life. I am so glad to have captured their stories, and in doing so, I have crystallized the lessons I have learned from each one of them. My dogs have been patient and loving. They have stood with me while I gathered the strength to take just one more step, whether it be to walk into my grief or find my voice and say "I will not live like this! I am moving forward."

Perhaps you, dear reader, are at a place in your life where you need healing, where you need to pull forth greater resilience than you think you have. Perhaps you share one or more of my disabilities. Perhaps you are in an unloving or even dangerous relationship. I pass on to you what my dogs have shared with me.

Dogged resilience is simply taking one step at a time.

And how fortunate for you if you have a canine friend, large or small, to push their nose into your hand. "I'm here," they remind you. "You are not alone."

From the Author

My Dogs And How They Shaped My Life is my first memoir.

This book fulfills the promise I made to myself in the second grade. I set a goal to publish a book based on my life experiences. This is it. I chose my dogs for my first book because I have had so many truly wonderful animals and no one will know them unless I write their stories down. It has been a labor of love.

What I didn't realize when I started was how deeply I had to reach inside myself to share some of my most vulnerable and valuable life experiences. I reflected on very difficult and debilitating experiences until I was able to shift my perspective to one that was both real and recovered. It was hard work. I learned a lot about resilience in the process. I hope you benefit from my story.

There's more information about Jude's amazing canines at

www.welldonepublishing.company

Read about:

- Lil Bear's adventure when captured and missing for five days
- Perfect Paddy's story of what happened that brutal Christmas at Phil's
- And more to come!

> **Jude + Lacey: Award Winner in Petco Foundation**
> **"Holiday Wishes" 2016 campaign**
> See their story at https://www.petcofoundation.org/love-story/jude-lacey/

Made in the USA
San Bernardino, CA
02 September 2018